PA
3??
L46
19?
TOMAN

DISCARD

D1509791

DISCARD

THE GREEK TRAGEDY
IN NEW TRANSLATIONS

GENERAL EDITORS
William Arrowsmith and Herbert Golder

EURIPIDES: Electra

EURIPIDES

Electra

Translated by
JANET LEMBKE
and
KENNETH J. RECKFORD

New York   Oxford
OXFORD UNIVERSITY PRESS
1994

Oxford University Press

Oxford New York Toronto
Delhi Bombay Calcutta Madras Karachi
Kuala Lumpur Singapore Hong Kong Tokyo
Nairobi Dar es Salaam Cape Town
Melbourne Auckland Madrid

and associated companies in
Berlin Ibadan

Copyright © 1994 by Janet Lembke and Kenneth J. Reckford

Published by Oxford University Press, Inc.
198 Madison Avenue, New York, New York 10016-4314

Oxford is a registered trademark of Oxford University Press

All rights reserved. No part of this publication
may be reproduced, stored in a retrieval system, or transmitted,
in any form or by any means, electronic, mechanical,
photocopying, recording, or otherwise, without the prior
permission of Oxford University Press

Library of Congress Cataloging-in-Publication Data
Euripides.
[Electra. English]
Electra / Euripides ; translated by Janet Lembke and Kenneth J. Reckford.
p. cm. — (The Greek tragedy in new transitions)
ISBN 0-19-508576-0 (pbk.)
1. Electra (Greek mythology)—Drama.
I. Title. II. Series.
PA3975.E5L46 1994
882'.01—dc20 93-3685

9 8 7 6 5 4 3
Printed in the United States of America

CHICAGO PUBLIC LIBRARY
TOMAN BRANCH
4005 W. 27th ST.   60623

EDITORS' FOREWORD

The Greek Tragedy in New Translations is based on the conviction that poets like Aeschylus, Sophocles, and Euripides can only be properly rendered by translators who are themselves poets. Scholars may, it is true, produce useful and perceptive versions. But our most urgent present need is for a *re-creation* of these plays—as though they had been written, freshly and greatly, by masters fully at home in the English of our own times. Unless the translator is a poet, his original is likely to reach us in crippled form: deprived of the power and pertinence it must have if it is to speak to us of what is permanent in the Greek. But poetry is not enough; the translator must obviously *know* what he is doing, or he is bound to do it badly. Clearly, few contemporary poets possess enough Greek to undertake the complex and formidable task of transplanting a Greek play without also "colonializing" it or stripping it of its deep cultural difference, its remoteness from us. And that means depriving the play of that crucial *otherness* of Greek experience—a quality no less valuable to us than its closeness. Collaboration between scholar and poet is therefore the essential operating principle of the series. In fortunate cases scholar and poet co-exist; elsewhere we have teamed able poets and scholars in an effort to supply, through affinity and intimate collaboration, the necessary combination of skills.

An effort has been made to provide the general reader or student with first-rate critical introductions, clear expositions of translators' principles, commentary on difficult passages, ample stage directions, and glossaries of mythical terms encountered in the plays. Our purpose throughout has been to make the reading of the plays as vivid as possible. But our poets have constantly tried to remember that they were translating *plays*—plays meant to be produced, in language that actors could speak, naturally and with dignity. The poetry aims at being *dramatic* poetry and realizing itself in words and actions that are both speakable and playable.

Finally, the reader should perhaps be aware that no pains have been spared in order that the "minor" plays should be translated as carefully and

v

brilliantly as the acknowledged masterpieces. For the Greek Tragedy in New Translations aims to be, in the fullest sense, *new*. If we need vigorous new poetic versions, we also need to see the plays with fresh eyes, to reassess the plays *for ourselves,* in terms of our own needs. This means translations that liberate us from the canons of an earlier age because the translators have recognized, and discovered, in often neglected works, the perceptions and wisdom that make these works ours and necessary to us.

A NOTE ON THE SERIES FORMAT

If only for the illusion of coherence, a series of thirty-three Greek plays requires a consistent format. Different translators, each with his individual voice, cannot possibly develop the sense of a single coherent style for each of the three tragedians; nor even the illusion that, despite their differences, the tragedians share a common set of conventions and a generic, or period, style. But they can at least share a common approach to orthography and a common vocabulary of conventions.

1. Spelling of Greek Names

Adherence to the old convention whereby Greek names were first Latinized before being housed in English is gradually disappearing. We are now clearly moving away from Latinization and toward precise transliteration. The break with tradition may be regrettable, but there is much to be said for hearing and seeing Greek names as though they were both Greek and *new,* instead of Roman or neo-classical importations. We cannot of course see them as wholly new. For better or worse certain names and myths are too deeply rooted in our literature and thought to be dislodged. To speak of "Helene" and "Hekabe" would be no less pedantic and absurd than to write "Aischylos" or "Platon" or "Thoukydides." There are of course borderline cases. "Jocasta" (as opposed to "Iokaste") is not a major mythical figure in her own right; her familiarity in her Latin form is a function of the fame of Sophocles' play as the tragedy *par excellence.* And as tourists we go to Delphi, not Delphoi. The precisely transliterated form may be pedantically "right," but the pedantry goes against the grain of cultural habit and actual usage.

As a general rule, we have therefore adopted a "mixed" orthography according to the principles suggested above. When a name has been firmly housed in English (admittedly the question of domestication is often moot), the traditional spelling has been kept. Otherwise names have been transliterated. Throughout the series the *-os* termination of masculine names has been adopted, and Greek diphthongs (as in Iphigene*ia*) have normally been retained. We cannot expect complete agreement from readers (or from translators, for that matter) about borderline cases. But we want at least to make the operative principle clear: to walk a narrow line between orthographical extremes in the hope of keeping what should not, if possible, be lost; and refreshing, in however tenuous a way, the specific sound and name-boundedness of Greek experience.

2. Stage directions

The ancient manuscripts of the Greek plays do not supply stage directions (though the ancient commentators often provide information relevant to staging, delivery, "blocking," etc.). Hence stage directions must be inferred from words and situations and our knowledge of Greek theatrical conventions. At best this is a ticklish and uncertain procedure. But it is surely preferable that good stage directions should be provided by the translator than that the reader should be left to his own devices in visualizing action, gesture, and spectacle. Obviously the directions supplied should be both spare and defensible. Ancient tragedy was austere and "distanced" by means of masks, which means that the reader must not expect the detailed intimacy ("He shrugs and turns wearily away," "She speaks with deliberate slowness, as though to emphasize the point," etc.) which characterizes stage directions in modern naturalistic drama. Because Greek drama is highly rhetorical and stylized, the translator knows that his words must do the real work of inflection and nuance. Therefore every effort has been made to supply the visual and tonal sense required by a given scene and the reader's (or actor's) putative unfamiliarity with the ancient conventions.

3. Numbering of lines

For the convenience of the reader who may wish to check the English against the Greek text or vice versa, the lines have been numbered according to both the Greek text and the translation. The lines of the English translation have been numbered in multiples of ten, and these numbers have been set in the right-hand margin. The (inclusive) Greek numeration will be found bracketed at the top of the page. The reader will doubtless note that in many plays the English lines out-number the Greek, but he should not therefore conclude that the translator has been unduly prolix. In most cases the reason is simply that the translator has adopted the free-flowing norms of modern Anglo-American prosody, with its brief, breath-and emphasis-determined lines, and its habit of indicating cadence and caesuras by line length and setting rather than by conventional punctuation. Other translators have preferred four-beat or five-beat lines, and in these cases Greek and English numerations will tend to converge.

4. Notes and Glossary

In addition to the Introduction, each play has been supplemented by Notes (identified by the line numbers of the translation) and a Glossary. The Notes are meant to supply information which the translators deem important to the interpretation of a passage; they also afford the translator an opportunity to justify what he has done. The Glossary is intended to spare the reader the trouble of going elsewhere to look up mythical or geographical terms. The entries are not meant to be comprehensive; when a fuller explanation is needed, it will be found in the Notes.

Boston   WILLIAM ARROWSMITH AND HERBERT GOLDER

CONTENTS

ELECTRA

INTRODUCTION

I

A revenge play gone askew, Shakespeare's *Hamlet* has misled numberless theatergoers, readers, and critics into seeking some definite answer to what seemed the obvious question: why doesn't Hamlet get on with the job? After Hamlet learns from his father's ghost how Claudius poisoned his brother the king and stole his queen-wife (Hamlet's mother), and after Hamlet confirms that tale by staging the play-murder and play-seduction, all he need do is kill his uncle. Surely Elsinor will support him, so why delay? Is it because Hamlet has a flawed character? Is he overly intellectual and given to melancholy brooding? Or is it because his Oedipal strivings lead him to identify unconsciously with Claudius?

All these possibilities may be correct, for Shakespeare gives wide scope to directors, actors, and critics to superimpose their own interpretation. But this odd tragedy of hesitation, of vengeance delayed, has other underlying motivations. Shakespeare's Hamlet is no hothead, no Laertes. He is a thoughtful, self-aware person in a thoughtless world. Uneasily he finds himself cast in what might have been—in what in an earlier period was— the typical revenge play, where the hero outwits and kills the usurper. Hamlet rushes into nothing. He probes and tests. Very sensibly he demands reassurances that his informant was an honest ghost, not a tempting devil. Wisely, too, he forbears killing a villain at his (seeming) prayers. Certainly his mind is clouded—by shock, by sexual disturbance, and by a madness only half feigned; it only clears in Act 5, when resolution is still outpaced by events. But he has also been *thinking* all this time—about himself, about family and friends, about Denmark, and about what Maynard Mack has called the "pervasive inscrutability" of things. It is not just that Hamlet is unready for revenge, but that, for this intelligent and sensitive hero, the call to revenge opens up a host of questions that require but do not receive a simple answer.

Euripides' *Electra,* by contrast, is a tragedy of nonhesitation.

3

Electra, if not Orestes, is entirely decisive, and the two accomplish their business of revenge with marvelous efficiency and ease. So why does this play (much more than *Hamlet*) leave such a bitter aftertaste?

To Euripides' audience the rightness of revenge at Argos must have seemed self-evident. It had almost scriptural authority, for Zeus himself, early in the *Odyssey*, cites Aigisthos' murder of Agamemnon as a paradigm of human wrongdoing and folly. Aigisthos was warned, says Zeus, but he ignored the warning, and was rightfully killed by Orestes, Agamemnon's son and avenger. Later, indeed, Orestes' revenge is held up to Telemachus as a model of right conduct, but fortunately Penelope proves faithful, unlike Clytemnestra, and so Odysseus enjoys a paradigmatically successful Return and Revenge (with disguise, reconnoitering, and various recognitions) and order is restored to Ithaca. By contrast, Orestes' revenge evolves into guilt and pain, for in post-Homeric lyric narrative and in Attic tragedy he must kill Clytemnestra as well as Aigisthos, bringing down a mother's Furies upon himself. And yet, with Apollo's and Athena's help he is purified and acquitted of crime, and the old rule of Mycenae is restored. Few Greeks can have doubted that Orestes' revenge, albeit painful, was finally necessary and right.

But Euripides, as ever, has doubts; and he continually forces us to consider the "pervasive inscrutability" of a world in which traditional mythic assumptions about the morality of revenge are contradicted by ordinary human feeling and experience. Yet Euripides' characters lag behind their author in sensibility. Orestes hesitates before killing his mother but remains feeble and irresolute; his stronger sister drives him on, even guiding his hand in the killing stroke. Like Hamlet, Electra is impulsive and more than a little mad, but she utterly lacks Hamlet's self-awareness (which emerges, not least, in flashes of sympathy with others). Instead, her moral and spiritual nearsightedness connives with the dark side of that inscrutable universe to create new evil. It is only after the last murder that Electra's and Orestes' eyes see clearly; only then do they acknowledge their deed, asking whether Apollo's oracle may have been a voice of evil.

With Electra, as with Hamlet, reductionist explanations are tempting. We can say that Electra has a father fixation, that she has become deranged through pathological grief and isolation. "She is quite mad," we say, a forerunner of that unattractive lunatic in the Strauss–von Hofmannsthal opera. But this is to evade the issue. For Euripides, like Shakespeare, shows us a world where good and bad people alike fail, and where the moral differences are not, in the end, so very clear. There is something wrong at bottom—and not just with Argos (or with Denmark). The time is out of joint.

The crucial theme in *Hamlet* is performance. Hamlet uses a troupe of players to test court appearances. He is also aware of himself as performing a part in a play where his understanding and control of things are inadequate, and where playing, rather than clarifying life, drives him deeper into chaos. By contrast, Electra puts on a performance as though it were her very skin. Her grievances and anger have become her life. She neither reflects nor gives Orestes the necessary time to reflect. Awareness comes too late, even though (like Hamlet) this brother and sister survive for what in another world might have been a happy ending.

II

Aeschylus' *Oresteia* (458 B.C.) told the later story of the House of Atreus in three consecutive plays, as in three acts. In *Agamemnon,* that hero returns triumphant from Troy with captives and spoils. Clytemnestra dominates the play; she has laid her plans carefully; she lures her captive, Agamemnon, into the palace, where he and Cassandra are killed. When the queen, on reemerging, proclaims and defends her act over the two bodies, and Aigisthos, the weak usurper, joins her, we feel how much the moral and political order has been subverted, and we can foretell that, despite Clytemnestra's prayer, the troubles of the House will not stop here. In *The Libation Bearers,* Orestes returns secretly. Aided by Electra and the chorus, he lures Aigisthos to death, then kills Clytemnestra. Apollo ordained these killings and will stand by Orestes, even though at the play's end Orestes turns to flight, pursued by the Furies. In *Eumenides* he comes to Athens, still pursued by the Furies and defended by Apollo; and in a cosmically decisive trial with human judges, but presided over by Athena, he is acquitted of murder. After the verdict Orestes goes off and Athena appeases the Furies, who are transformed into the Eumenides, "benevolent" underworld deities.

The *Oresteia* moves through suffering to release. It offers no easy moral: "Great tragedy," as someone has said, "is closer to the altar than the pulpit"; but there is a discernable movement from complication to resolution, from division (especially male vs. female) to reconciliation, from darkness to light, and from servitude to freedom. The entanglements of the cursed House, evoked in choral song and in Cassandra's darkly visionary pronouncements, are given their full weight of tragic repetition, of crime breeding crime. It began with Tantalos, the arch-sinner, who served up his son Pelops to the gods. (Pelops was saved, only his shoulder was replaced with ivory. He grew up to seize the rich kingdom of Mycenae by fraud and violence.) Atreus, Pelops' son, struggled with his brother Thyestes for sovereignty; his unfaithful wife, Aerope, connived with Thyestes, but Atreus regained power and served up Thyestes' two older children to him at a banquet ("Thyestes' Feast"). A third son, Aigisthos, seduced Clytemnestra and joined with her to kill Agamemnon (who had incurred further guilt by sacrificing his daughter, Iphigenia, leading Greeks to die at Troy, and sacking that city's holy shrines). So when Orestes in turn stands over the two bodies, we have to ask: Will the chain of disasters ever be broken?" The trilogy, through its last act, gives a positive answer. Not an easy one: for much remains unsettled, and there are hints of arbitrary violence underlying the establishment of human and divine justice; yet, at both levels, a satisfying resolution is achieved. The law court, divinely sanctioned, supplants the vendetta. The very spirits of blood-vengeance are transformed. Whether at Athens or upon Olympus, progress comes violently and painfully, but it does come.

I return to *The Libation Bearers*, that second act against which Euripides' *Electra* is specifically played. The play's first movement is from mourning to recognition. Orestes enters with his faithful friend Pylades; he watches as Electra and the chorus of servingwomen bear ritual offerings to the tomb, mourn for Agamemnon, and cry out for help and vengeance. Electra discovers signs: a lock of hair, a footprint like her brother's. Has he really come? She wavers between hope and despair; but quickly and joyfully—and with a third, finally convincing recognition-token, a piece of her weaving—Orestes reveals himself to her. He is confident of Apollo's backing but driven also by a threat of Hell—his father's Furies, if he fails to avenge him. The second movement is lyrical, intense. The chorus, Orestes, and Electra pray to the powers of heaven, the underworld, and the dead man (his will is still potent, only needing to be aroused). Power and right, they and we feel, are on their side. Vengeance follows, with trickery. Orestes, posing as a stranger, brings a false story of his own death. Aigisthos arrives. He is directed inside and killed. Clytemnestra realizes her danger, calls for an axe (she is still dangerous), but Orestes stops her. She pleads for mercy; he hesitates; and Pylades, heretofore silent, urges him on in three tremendous verses that might have been spoken by Apollo himself. Orestes drags Clytemnestra inside, to kill her. Now the chorus celebrates. "Justice guided his hand." "Now we can see the light." Orestes comes out, displays the two bodies, and reaffirms the justice of his actions, guided by Apollo. As he departs, pursued by the Furies, for Delphi and Athens, the chorus awards him final praise—though it also asks, "Where will it end?"

Taken in isolation, *The Libation Bearers* is an exercise in fear. We keep watch in the shadow of one murder, waiting, like Clytemnestra, for another. Old anger exacts new vengeance with almost ritual precision. It is harsh and frightening, and we sense more suffering to come; but Aeschylus allows little doubt about the necessity of Orestes' act. Apollo ordained it; Apollo will see the process through. And retributive justice (*dikē*), once completed, will restore the light of freedom to Argos. The chorus is reassured and reassuring. Electra, a sympathetic figure, leaves the stage mid-way. All Orestes need do is act, suffer, and endure. Neither he nor his acts of killing are finally isolated; all signs point to a larger pattern of meaning, and of redemption. In Euripides' *Electra* things will seem less clear.

III

As a single play, Euripides' *Electra* isolates the killing of Aigisthos and Clytemnestra from any larger, Aeschylean development. We are not shown their past wrongdoings at firsthand, nor do we watch as powerful deities negotiate a more promising future. The action is entirely human until the epilogue. As in Aeschylus' *Libation Bearers* (though not in Sophocles' *Electra*), it builds to the emotionally more disturbing murder of Clytemnestra; but Euripides gives Electra a large share in this killing, somewhat replaying the earlier Clytemnestra and isolating for us the merely human question: What sort of persons, and in what frame of mind, would kill their mother?

But first, a surprise. The scene is shifted: away from palace and tomb, into a pleasant country setting among distant hills. The prologue introducing the play's first movement (ll. 1–447) gives largely familiar mythic background, but with a twist: it is delivered by the Farmer to whom Electra has been married off in order to make her potential offspring ineffective. The rural setting conveys Electra's double isolation, of body (she considers this exile) and of spirit. Her life is unnatural. She is a princess turned farmer's wife, a maiden married in name only. At the same time, the somewhat idealized ordinariness of country life—here represented by the decent, gentle-natured Farmer, the chorus of cheerful young women of the neighborhood, and (later in the play) a faithful old retainer—shows up with irony and humor every false note in the world of tragic heroics that Electra constantly invokes. Aeschylean conventions that once supported high tragedy now prove impotent. The old revenge plot forfeits its accustomed nobility, its basic rightness. What remains is altogether perverse.

In *Hamlet* the hero's suit of inky black, though incongruous at the bright court, was justified. It was the others who had, too quickly, forgotten the dead. Hamlet's performance rings true, as theirs does not. By contrast, as we watch Electra's act with cropped hair and water-jar on head and as we hear her voice her grievances, we come to feel, together with the patient Farmer, that this has been going on for years. It all belongs, so to speak, in some tragic opera—not here in the beneficent countryside. As the Farmer points out, with very gentle irony, Electra need not draw water on his account: they do have help; and if she insists—well, it isn't very far to the spring, anyway. And then there are those friendly young women who invite Electra to join them in celebrating Hera's festival. Her refusal, her insistence on mourning, might seem understandable, even after all those years; but when she relapses into complaints ("I *never* go out, I *never* have anything to wear. If I didn't make all my own clothes, I would go *naked!*"), we cannot help remembering how the chorus offered to lend her party dresses and jewelry a few minutes earlier. Her isolation from society, even from the gods, is partly of her own making.

Orestes, too, seems out of place in this quiet setting. His business should have been at the palace. He is not the strong Aeschylean hero, moving prudently, steadily, and confidently toward his divinely ordained goal; still less is he the swan-knight of Electra's dreams who will return to rescue her from all this. "My courageous brother," she will say indignantly, would never "crawl here in secret" for fear of Aigisthos—but that is exactly what Orestes has done. From the first, he is timid, indecisive. He is prepared to skip across the border if things go badly. On seeing the "slave girl" he panics. Even after eavesdropping and discovering that she is Electra, he still hesitates for an intolerably long time, telling her a false story, and saying things like "Oh, dear" and "What would Orestes say?" as she goes through her Cinderella performance. When the Farmer returns, his straightforward hospitality shows up Orestes by contrast as a snobbish, patronizing young aristocrat who, underneath all those pseudosophisticated comments on true nobility, may be deeply insecure. Orestes goes on and on, playing for time. By contrast, the Farmer exhibits a gentleman's naturalness and ease, even when, in a very funny scene, Electra scolds him for inviting important people to dinner when he knows they don't have enough food.

Both sister and brother play a self-conscious part. Electra, especially, plays to the gallery: to the gods, to show how much she is mistreated; to the "absent" Orestes, to convey how greatly Agamemnon and his children are abused. And Orestes, though less intelligent, is also disingenuous. In a deeper sense, neither one is self-aware. Each is caught up in a performance that, in this country setting, must seem unnatural and artificial. The dissonance is often comic; there is more laughter to come. It undercuts our expected sympathy with this tragic pair. More important, it helps Euripides distort the revenge plot into something unnatural and evil. At the same time, it relaxes our minds and sensibilities, much as Shakespeare's lighter scenes can do, so that we are caught off guard when, finally, the kitchen knife is set to the victim's throat.

IV

The second movement of *Electra* (ll. 448–903) carries us through a happy recognition and a successful act of revenge, each culminating in a high moment of hope and joy.

After a choral ode pits mythic good against evil, culminating in the prophetic threat that Clytemnestra will pay in blood for her evildoing, the Old Man's entrance starts a comic scene. His ordinariness, his slow climb, his presents of food and drink, including a lamb, return us to that cheerful, relaxed mood in which high tragedy must seem misplaced. (This lamb will contrast wonderfully with the Golden Lamb, legendary emblem of rivalry, seduction, and murder.) A hilarious failure of Aeschylean recognition-tokens follows. The lock of hair, the footprint, the piece of child's weaving—all are demolished scornfully by Electra, who is well armored against false hope; but then the Old Man sees the scar on Orestes' forehead and reveals his identity. We might wonder why Electra never noticed it. Perhaps she was preoccupied. Or we might think of Homer, of the scar on Odysseus' thigh that gives him away to the nurse, and almost to Penelope. It was inflicted by a wild boar, in Odysseus' adolescent *rite de passage*. (The Homeric echo goes with many others, such as Odysseus' stay with the good swineherd before he comes to the palace, to kill the suitors.) But where did Orestes' scar come from? He fell, chasing a pet deer around the yard. It all seems rather silly. Orestes is no Odysseus. Nor is he the gleaming savior of Electra's dreams.

Their reunion is nonetheless joyful, a high moment marked by embraces and by choral dance and song. But it is brief. Orestes turns quickly to planning revenge. How to attack Aigisthos? The diffident hero is easily discouraged by obstacles ("You can't even get *near* the palace!"). He snatches eagerly at the Old Man's suggestion that he catch Aigisthos in the open, at sacrifice. With stronger determination and a power of command ironically reminiscent of the Aeschylean Clytemnestra, Electra announces that *she* will deal with her mother. It will be easy to trap and kill her, playing on her pity. After brief prayers (they will seem perfunctory, indeed, to anyone who recalls the great invocation scene in Aeschylus), the troops depart. Electra proclaims "Victory or Death." With a sure sense of melodrama, she will hold a sword in readiness against bad news.

The intervening time is marked by a second choral ode, less bright and happy this time: the crimes of the House, centering on that Golden Lamb, culminate in Clytemnestra's murder of Agamemnon. Even as they sing, the treacherous Aigisthos is being killed by Orestes. And what a killing it is! The messenger's report is a masterpiece of black humor. Even Aigisthos, it seems, is not like Aigisthos: we never see him for ourselves, but he is described as an amiable, easygoing person who, on seeing the strangers, quickly invites them to join in the sacrifice and feast. (Agamemnon, in Homer's version, was slaughtered at a feast.) We may be deceived; that smiling villain, Claudius, could be genial too. Still, the abuse of hospitality is unsettling; and, still more, the perversion of sacrificial ritual. Hamlet had better intentions when he declined to kill Claudius at his prayers. Orestes has no such scruples; it is enough for him to keep his hands unwashed. Invited to show his skill with the cleaver, he smashes it down (attacking from the rear, of course) through his host's backbone. It all works splendidly, and without time for reflection, we are caught up in the general mood of celebration as the chorus proclaims victory, joy, and hope. It is the last happy moment in the play.

V

The third and climactic movement of *Electra* (ll. 904–1276) begins with a moral descent. Orestes and Pylades enter, to be crowned with wreaths like victorious athletes; and before we know it, Electra is insulting Aigisthos' corpse. However justified her hatred, this is clearly hubris, on a par with Aigisthos' insults to Agamemnon's tomb reported earlier. Even the chorus seems uneasy, although it reaffirms the justice of this revenge. Victory is losing its moral luster. And then, appropriately, Clytemnestra is sighted, and Orestes asks in panic, "What should we do? Must we kill our mother?"

This is (differently from Aeschylus' staged confrontation of Orestes and Clytemnestra) the decisive scene. We feel the pressures. Orestes knows what a mother is; he cries out that Apollo's bidding must be wrong. (Is it "a damned ghost that we have seen?") What forces him on is not Pylades this time, speaking awesomely for the god, but Electra's iron will. She feels no qualms, parries every objection. We sense the tension within her: to hesitate now is to lose everything. Her final, most effective appeal is to Orestes' manhood. Ironically, he is overborne by a woman—precisely as Aigisthos had been (in Electra's own contemptuous words). Orestes gives in, although, as he says, killing is no longer sport. He goes in, to await his second victim.

A fanfare of trumpets, and Clytemnestra enters in her carriage with a rich entourage. (Today it would be a long black chauffeured limousine.) Although the scene echoes that other famous scene of Agamemnon's return and moral entrapment, we are meant to see what Electra cannot, that Clytemnestra is a person, a woman who has aged and weakened and may even feel remorse. (Impressions are subjective, but we were told earlier, in the prologue, that she once saved Electra's life.) All the same, the lady protests too much. Her overrehearsed arguments seem unconvincing: how Agamemnon killed Iphigenia in a bad cause; how he brought a mistress, Cassandra, home with him. She even tries humor, appeals to female solidarity against irresponsible males. But Electra has taken on her mother's earlier hardness. Her rebuttal (surely also much rehearsed) is cold, sarcastic, brilliantly effective. She strips away her mother's pretenses, to reveal the shameful adulteress, destroyer of family bonds. Yet her intense anger is there, and once she almost gives away the game:

> . . . And if blood
> calls for blood in the name of Justice, I will kill you—
> I and your son Orestes—to avenge our father.
>
> (*stepping back*)
>
> If death was just there, here it is also just.
>
> (ll. 1130–33)

At the last moment she covers her tracks with commonplaces.

We might (if we listened thoughtfully) be surprised when Clytemnestra answers with soft words. Her forbearance, her genuine sorrow, might even lead us to see her as a person, to ask why, after all, she must be killed. But Electra refuses to listen, or to look. "Too late to lament. There's no cure now" (l. 1146). She forces a quarrel, angers her mother, and makes her hurry inside—Clytemnestra now wanting, with understandable impatience, to be done with this wretched scene and (more irony here) to rejoin her husband at the sacrifice.

So she goes in. Electra follows. And Clytemnestra is killed, very quickly, even while the chorus recalls the killing of Agamemnon and asserts once more that justice has been carried out. But when the killers reappear, spattered with blood, everyone sees what has happened as though for the first time. Orestes foresees an exile, Electra an isolation, far worse than before. They see, and lead us to imagine, the killing as it really happened: Clytemnestra's plea; Orestes' driving his sword through her living flesh, in a horrible parody of Perseus and the Gorgon; Electra's guiding his hand. "Too late to lament," Electra had said. "There's no cure now." With sorrow and respect, they cover the body; and Electra asks (we have a sense of déjà vu) that the ills of the House end here.

VI

We may ask, at this moment of retrospection just before the epilogue, how the actions, songs, and judgments of the chorus should themselves be judged. Have these sympathetic young women become accomplices, even cheerleaders, in the actions of revenge? They have helped lure the last victim and have helped justify (and obscure) new killings by keeping old ones before our eyes. To put it simply, they believe that they are living in an Aeschylean world where *dikē* (justice, payment for wrongdoing, satisfaction rendered) is gradually reinstituted under the supervision of heaven. Even after Electra abuses Aigisthos' corpse, they perceive his dreadful fate as balancing his dreadful deeds. So, too, they invoke measure for measure as Clytemnestra is killed. Only afterward does their judgment shift (like ours?), and only in part: to decry the ongoing misery of the House and to blame Electra, as she now blames herself, for the evil she willed earlier and for her dreadful compulsion of her brother.

Our imagination, like that of the chorus, has traveled far since that first lovely ode with Achilles' ships escorted to Troy by leaping dolphins and dancing Nereids; with Chiron, the good centaur, who nurtured that prince of heroes; with the blazing sun and dancing stars, emblems of brilliance and cosmic order, at the center of Achilles' shield; and with depictions of legendary combats, Perseus and the Gorgon, Bellerophon (on Pegasus) and the Chimaera. In this familiar world of bright heroes slaying monsters killing is easily justified, and the chorus looks forward confidently to a time when the avenging sword of justice will let blood from Clytemnestra's throat.

On closer inspection, recent critics have argued, the ode betrays hints of latent violence and of the dusty death to which even great Homeric heroes come. What matters more is our growing sense of a discrepancy between the traditional, somewhat romanticized world of heroic legend and the quite ordinary life of the Argive uplands where Electra and now Orestes find themselves. The contrast makes for surprise and laughter. It may also shock an audience into facing human realities. In legend Perseus' killing of the Gorgon Medusa was a victory of humanity, backed by bright gods, over dark and monstrous evil. Accordingly, in Aeschylus' *Libation Bearers,* the chorus urges the unseen Orestes to "hold the heart of Perseus in your bosom" and to kill Clytemnestra blamelessly, as one might a "loathsome Gorgon" (ll. 827–37). But in Euripides' play, after Orestes (aided by Electra) kills Clytemnestra in the manner of Perseus, holding a cloak before his eyes as he stabs her flesh, the difference between slaying a monster and murdering one's mother becomes appallingly clear.

In the second choral ode (ll. 724–71), myth approaches history. Once again Euripides begins with images of loveliness, of music and pastoral beauty; but the Golden Lamb, emblem of sovereignty, soon becomes a symbol of deception, violence, and cruel revenge—of wrong breeding wrong. Thyestes' seduction of Atreus' wife Aerope, his deceitful seizure of power, foreshadow Aigisthos' seduction of Clytemnestra and their murder of Agamemnon; Thyestes' horrific fall (not here detailed) should have been a lesson to Clytemnestra, had she "remembered." But memories are selective. So are interpretations of myth, and of history. Even as the chorus sings of justice rendered, its own interpretation of things is selective and misleading; and so, perhaps, is ours.

When Zeus, in this second ode, turned back the sun, was he confirming Atreus' rule despite the stolen lamb? Or was he proclaiming universal horror at the escalation of evil, the unnaturalness of "Thyestes' Feast?" We do not know. The chorus, less naive than earlier, professes skepticism.

Still, it seems more than ordinarily portentous when the sun, that fixed center of brightness and order, alters his course. The world is changed and, in this version, changed forever. Which is to say, that the time in which the chorus sings, and in which we live, is still, radically, out of joint; and there is little chance that further killing in the name of justice will set it right.

VII

Although the stage is thick with corpses at the end of *Hamlet,* the ending brings some consolation, some promise of order. Horatio will live to report Hamlet's story aright. Fortinbras proclaims his nobility. There is a suggestion that, with the usurper dead, the poisonous corruption of Denmark has been expelled; perhaps Hamlet served as sacrificial victim so that the state might return to normality and health. The cannons shot off now to honor the dead prince, not to amuse a drunken usurper, seem finally reassuring.

The epilogue of *Electra,* by contrast, is intentionally somewhat lame. Certainly, the Dioskouroi mean well. Castor, their spokesman, tries to bring us back into an Aeschylean world of meaning and resolution, and even to provide a happy ending all around; but his effort somewhat miscarries, raising more questions than it solves. Castor gives the impression of a decent but minor figure in the heavenly bureaucracy who, although disapproving privately, cannot criticize the misjudgments of his superior, Apollo, in public. Needless to say, nothing like a convincing Aeschylean theodicy is forthcoming.

Certainly, Castor tries. He tells how Orestes, pursued by the Furies, will travel to Delphi for purification and to Athens for acquittal (which is familiar and Aeschylean); how Electra will marry Pylades; how the Farmer will be rewarded. But where are the civic and cosmic solutions, so familiar from Aeschylus? There is no suggestion that Orestes will return to Argos, that the old political order (did it ever exist?) will be restored. As for divinity: the Furies must be subdued in this version, not appeased; nor is it reassuring to learn of Zeus only that he planned the Trojan War to solve the population problem. That Helen is absolved of guilt (for human beings may be pardoned their blind actions in an irrational world) seems less than consoling.

All Castor wants is to finish his prepared speech on an upbeat note of promised happiness and release from toil (ll. 1284–1337), and then, not waiting for questions, to move on to the next crisis on the Sicilian Sea. He does not get off so easily. First Orestes and then Electra pose unanswerable questions. Why all this horror? Why couldn't the Dioskouroi have helped their sister Clytemnestra? It was Apollo, says Castor, and fate, and the accumulated disasters of the House of Atreus binding their victims in common misfortune. Whether or not they accept these answers, the human actors now turn to each other one last time to share their sorrow and their love. What awaits them is pain, separation, and unending exile. Castor looks on with pity, too, even though he closes on a new authoritative note: The good are rewarded by heaven; the bad are left to their misery. The chorus comments on this in the play's last words: happy the life that does not sink beneath misfortune.

What are we left with, finally, when the actors and chorus have departed? With less reassurance, surely, than at the end of *Hamlet* when the cannons shoot. For we have not, despite Castor's valiant efforts, been restored to that Aeschylean world where patterns of meaning, growth, and justice can be discerned behind human suffering, and where the order, not just of the polis but of the very gods, evolves over time and space. But neither are we in the world of Sophocles, where heroes and heroines struggle with intolerable loneliness and pain, yet achieve final nobility and worth, and sometimes even victory, through endurance and the paradoxical connivance of amoral gods. The heroine of Sophocles' *Electra* is difficult (like Antigone) but thoroughly admirable. She endures; she rejects oppression and helplessness; she will act, if only by herself—but Orestes, who counterfeited his own death, has returned alive to kill Clytemnestra and Aigisthos (in that order; the agony is not here, but in Electra's prolonged horror of loneliness and despair). Perhaps—we do not know— Sophocles' play came first. If so, Euripides wrote against *two* predecessors, degrading Sophocles' heroine while restressing, more finally than Aeschylus, the evil of matricide. Or perhaps Sophocles wrote last, to vindicate human nobility (as ever) under extreme pressure. Whatever the order, the contrast remains impressive: between the integrity of heroism in Sophocles, which challenges us to become greater than we are, and the disintegration, the sheer vulnerability of character and human life in Euripides, who insists on our basic helplessness to do anything lastingly great or good.

What Euripides leaves us with is compassion, the keener for lost reassurances. We learn to pity not just Agamemnon's mistreated children but also the ruinous adulterers, killers, and usurpers. This is not to forget that Aigisthos and Clytemnestra are dangerous still. They set their spies, hold Electra suspect, and would kill Orestes if they caught him returning to Argos. But more than that, they are vulnerable, like ourselves. Their flesh is weak, and their blood, once shed like an animal's, cannot be recalled. In the end, the common fate of mortals unites them beyond the passing distinctions of good and bad, noble and base, right and wrong.

It remains true that the pity evoked by our shared humanity can be ineffective, delusory, or positively dangerous as a guide to action, especially when it comes too late, as it so often does in Euripides' plays. Electra especially uses pity as a weapon: to spur Orestes on, to lure Clytemnestra to her doom. And when Orestes speaks of the heightened sensitivity from which uncommon people like himself must necessarily suffer—

> Harsh words. My god, how just hearing of miseries
> endured by others can sink sharp teeth into a man. . . .
> Pity, impossible for lowborn brutes, comes
> only to those who inherit noble feelings.
> But even they pay dearly to scruple overmuch.
>
> (ll. 302–3, 306–8)

We might reflect, if we had time, not just that Orestes' talk rings hollow, but that the world's wrongs might not be healed even today by that heightened sense of compassion that Euripidean tragedy still evokes in educated people like ourselves. It never was easy to do good.

Nevertheless, the ending of *Electra* speaks powerfully for the importance of pity, if not for its everyday efficacy. For even if the Dioskouroi arrive late and accomplish little, they still bring with them some heavenly brightness, and some binding up of wounds; and it is no small consolation that the gods themselves feel pity, not scorn, for human suffering;

> Pain, such pain in your words that even
> gods hear its anguish.
> I and my heavenly kind know
> pity for men who must suffer and die.
>
> (ll. 1374–77)

Castor's Olympian perspective briefly suggests what Euripides' spectators might have felt, or might have been meant to feel, as they looked down from their benches in the theater of Dionysos on the victims turned killers and the killers turned victims. And perhaps, from out of the anger and hatred, the bitterness and sharp divisions of war-torn Athens, they might momentarily have imagined what it would have been like to live in a kinder, happier world, where the ordinary gifts of life such as wine, cheese, lamb, and flowers shine with new beauty, and where, in Virgil's later words (and he was much influenced by Euripides) "there are tears for things, and the common fate of men touches the heart" (*sunt lacrimae rerum et mentem mortalia tangunt*).

VIII

Pleasure and pain kissed: for Euripides' audience, as it was brought through a "pleasure of many tears" (*polydakryn hadonan*) by the playwright's art; and again, just now, for ourselves as translators. To read Euripides closely means to become increasingly aware of the fragility of human life, and of the human spirit. But we also experienced what is too easily forgotten, the sheer excitement of the play as a play—its pace, surprises, and musicality, its sureness of artistic construction and effect—as we rehearsed Greek verses back and forth in the summer greenness of Chapel Hill or on a porch, refreshed by the sea breeze, in Beaufort, North Carolina.

It is never easy for *readers* to catch Euripides' interplay of joy and pain. When, for example, the chorus invites Electra to Hera's festival, the joyful rhythms of the many-voiced invitation bring out, by contrast, Electra's stark isolation, and her refusal in turn recalls the real possibility of human happiness from which she feels forever excluded. Or again: the beauty and joy of the "Nereid" lyrics is not just delusory, not just a foil to everyday unhappiness and failure. Joy is as real as pain. Knowledge of joy, or of the possibility of joy, enhances our sympathy for suffering and misfortune, even the extreme wretchedness into which Euripides' heroines and heroes are so regularly cast.

Our shared sense, as translators, of the pace, structure, and impact of *Electra* has been reinforced greatly by two dramatic readings: first, by Theater Wagon of Staunton, Virginia, in August 1986, directed by Rick Hite and produced in the generously theatrical house of Margaret and Fletcher Collins; and, second, by the UNC Playmakers of Chapel Hill, directed by David Hammond, in January 1987. A good dramatic reading opens one's eyes—and ears and feelings—to much. This is not to argue that modern recreations can *prove* anything about ancient plays. We could not prove (to take a difficult problem) that Aigisthos' head was separated from his body—though it *works*. But we did see things that the casual reader ignores, like the stage presence of the silent, sinister, masked Pylades accompanying Orestes, and the way he is echoed by the silent, masked Pollux accompanying Castor in the epilogue. Much, too, that we had sensed in the reading emerged strongly and clearly in performance: Orestes' athletic handsomeness; Electra's edge of hysteria; the Farmer's quiet dignity and humor, shared with the audience in an easy, familiar way; the broad comedy of the scene when the Old Man prowls around Orestes, peering at him, to his great disquiet; the *still* audible shock of the audience when Electra calls her mother a slut. We could go on. But, above all, these dramatic readings confirmed and enhanced our impression of how the play *moves,* in two senses. For Euripides takes us rapidly and masterfully through numerous quick scenes of wide-ranging contrasts, which not only surprise but also throw us constantly off balance; and we, the translators, who knew what was coming, felt silenced and shocked as much as the others by the killing of Clytemnestra when it came, and by the grief, the remorse, and the universal feeling of human pain in the last scenes. It is, even more than we realized, an extremely disturbing play.

What is also remarkable is how not just the sedentary translators but the directors and actors felt that they were in the hands of a master. We remember, admiringly, that Euripides was more than a playwright. He was director, producer, choreographer, and musical director. It takes many hands to do the job today, and our usual failure to recreate the singing, dancing, and music of *Electra*, as of other Greek tragedies, inevitably results in a considerable loss of pleasure, balance, and overall effectiveness.

It remains to give thanks. Our explorations of *Electra* were eased by James Diggle's fine new (1981) Oxford Classical Text of Euripides, Volume 2, which we mainly follow; by the still invaluable 1939 commentary of J. D. Denniston; by many outstanding articles and chapters on *Electra*;[1] and by the advice and encouragement of John Herington and David Kovacs. Gifted graduate students at Chapel Hill joined us in attacking textual and interpretive problems. We are grateful, too, for the watchful care of our twin editors, William Arrowsmith and Herbert Golder, as they continue to protect "The Greek Tragedy in New Translations" from untimely shipwreck.

A longer debt is to our spouses, who stood by us and encouraged us through this enterprise, and sometimes made fun of us. To Adrian Stanley and (now) to the memory of Mary Reckford, who died in November, we dedicate this translation.

Great Neck Point, N.C.   J.L.
Chapel Hill, N.C.   K.J.R.
March 1988

---

1. We single out as especially helpful the work of James Halporn, Katherine King, Masaaki Kubo, Michael O'Brien, Friedrich Solmsen, George Walsh, and Froma Zeitlin. Ann Michelini's newly published *Euripides and the Tragic Tradition* (1987) includes the best chapter on *Electra* we have seen.

ELECTRA

CHARACTERS

FARMER Electra's husband

ELECTRA

ORESTES Electra's brother

PYLADES a mute character, Orestes' friend and son of Orestes' protector Strophios

CHORUS of young, unmarried peasant women

OLD MAN former tutor to Agamemnon

MESSENGER Orestes' servant

CLYTEMNESTRA mother of Electra and Orestes, widow of Agamemnon

THE DIOSKOUROI Castor and Polydeukes, sons of Zeus, brothers of Clytemnestra

Servants to the Farmer
Men attending Orestes and Pylades
Trojan slave-women attending Clytemnestra

Line numbers in the right-hand margin of the text refer to the English translation only, and the Notes at p. 77 are keyed to these lines. The bracketed line numbers in the running headlines refer to the Greek text.

A farm in the mountains of Argos. In the background center, a small farmhouse.

The FARMER *enters from the farmhouse.*

FARMER   Age-old valley of my shining land, how your rivers
gleamed as they saw war launched in a thousand ships
when Lord Agamemnon sailed against Troy.
And after he'd killed Troy's ruler, Priam,
and burnt and leveled that famous city,
he came back to Argos to hang many spoils
seized from those barbarians high on our temple walls.
Away from home he found good luck, but in his own house
he was killed by Clytemnestra's treachery
and the hand of Thyestes' son Aigisthos.   10

A long line of kingship was broken when he died.
Now Aigisthos wears the country's crown
and holds both Agamemnon's scepter and his wife.
When the king sailed for Troy, he left at home
the baby Orestes and his little girl Electra.
Orestes would have died by Aigisthos' hand,
but his father's old tutor smuggled him away
and gave him to Strophios in the north for protection.
Electra stayed in her father's house.
When her youth reached its flower,   20
the foremost young men of Greece came courting.
But, terrified that she'd bear princely sons
to avenge Agamemnon, he held her under house arrest,
Aigisthos did, and denied her any marriage.

Yet, when he planned to kill her out of great fear
that she might take a highborn lover in secret
and bear him sons, her mother—a savage woman—
did save her from Aigisthos' hand. Reason is,
Clytemnestra had excuses for her husband's death
but dreaded blame for murdering her children.   30
Aigisthos answered with a new design:
by public decree he offered gold to the man

21

who'd kill Agamemnon's fugitive son.
Then he gave me young Electra to have
as my wife. My forefathers, Mycenean, highborn—
in them I can't be faulted, for my lineage
shines though we never had much money, a fact
that puts paid to the benefits of noble birth.
So, to sap the power of his fear, he gave her
      to me, a powerless man.   40
You see, if she'd married someone of position, he would have
waked Agamemnon's murder from its sleep, and then
Aigisthos would have paid the penalty.
Yet I never—Aphrodite, bear me witness—
never shamed Electra's bed. She is still virgin.
It would shame me, a man born poor,
to do such outrage to any rich man's girl.
It hurts to think that my kin in name only,
Orestes the exile, might come back to Argos
and find his unlucky sister married to me.   50

But anyone who says I'm foolish—receiving
a virgin in my house but not once touching her—
uses a worthless standard to take the measure
of self-control, and he's the fool.

        ELECTRA, *bearing a water-jar on her head, enters*
                           from the farmhouse.

ELECTRA Black night, brood-nurse of golden stars,
wrapped in your darkness I walk bearing this jar
to draw fresh water from the spring,
but not because need bends me to such menial work.
No! I'd show the gods how Aigisthos insults me.
And I cry my grief through wide air to my father.   60
Listen! Tyndareos' daughter—my mother
      who spoils all she touches—
drove me from home and heritage to please her new
husband. She slept beside him, bore him other children.
She casts Orestes and me from our own house.

FARMER My poor lady, why wear yourself out for me?
You weren't brought up for heavy labor.
Why not listen when I tell you let it be?

ELECTRA You are a friend I respect as I do the gods,
for in my troubles you have not once mocked me.   70
What providence for anyone beset by ills
to find a healing comfort such as you.
So, at no one's bidding, I *must* use my strength
to make your labors lighter, easier, and share
the work. You have more than enough to do
out there in the fields. Keeping house is my domain.
And when a working man comes in at dusk,
he likes to find order and his supper ready.

FARMER Go then, if that's what you want. The spring's not far.
Soon as daylight comes, I'll yoke the oxen,   80
drive them to the fields, and get on with planting.
No man can keep himself alive by mouthing
idle prayers to the gods. It takes hard work.

ELECTRA *and the* FARMER *exeunt to spring and fields,*
respectively.

ORESTES *and* PYLADES *enter with their attendants.*

ORESTES Pylades, you are the one man on this earth
I count as loyal—my friend, my host. You alone,
of all my friends, continued to admire me
when I suffered, as I still do, from the deadly
acts of my father's killer and my mother
        who spoils all she touches.
Now I come from Apollo's oracle at Delphi.   90
He ordered me home, where no one suspects my presence,
to exchange murder for my father's murder.
So, last night I went to my father's tomb,
wept, offered a fresh-clipped lock of hair,
and cut a sheep's throat over the altar,
all without being caught by those who lord it here.

Nor do I mean to set foot inside city walls.
Two goals, clear in sight, keep me near the border—
one, swift access to a safer country
if some king's man should spy me out;   100
the second, finding my sister—they say she lives
married to someone, she's no longer maiden.
I'd plan and work revenge with her, and through her
learn exactly what goes on inside those walls.

Sun's coming up—time to change course and leave
this path well used by daytime travelers.
Some man off ploughing his fields, some housemaid
at her errands might be able to tell us
if my sister lives anywhere near.

Look, here comes a servant,   110
jar of water on her shorn head—
somebody's slave. Pylades, let's find
a place to sit. We may overhear some
answers to the questions that brought me home.

ORESTES, PYLADES, *and their attendants conceal them-*
selves to eavesdrop.

ELECTRA *enters bearing a jar of water on her head and*
keening.

ELECTRA *(singing and dancing)*
Speed your step, season I wait for, O
come quickly, come wailing, come howling grief!
    Come now, now!
I was fathered by Agamemnon,
born to a queen, Clytemnestra,
a woman inviting hate.   120
Now citizens add "poor thing"
to Electra's name.
Cruel, how cruel my troubles!
How hateful my life!
Father who lies in death's darkness

your wife and Aigisthos made you their sacrifice—
        O Agamemnon.

Come, raise the dirge from its ghostworld.
Lead into light the pleasure of tears.

Speed your step, season I wait for, O   130
come quickly, come wailing, come howling grief!
        Come now, now!
City or household—where
has wandering led you, poor brother,
leaving a grief-stricken sister
locked fast in the women's rooms
of her father's house?
Return, put an end to my troubles,
release me from grief.
God, O God, stop your wandering. Come home   140
to Argos, to our murdered father's blood.
        Help me avenge him.

ELECTRA *takes the water-jar from her head and puts it on
the ground. As she sings and dances, she enacts the ges-
                            tures of mourning mentioned.*

Down with this weight that I carry, for only
at dawn can I cry out the dirges
        that catch in my throat night-long.
Wailing, words, the full music of death—
Father, to you in the dark earth
all of my body sings dirges.
Day after day I offer
tears pouring out and fingernails   150
raking my cheeks till they bleed,
hands gripping a head shorn of hair
        because you are dead.

                                    (*beating her head*)

        Drum, my hands, drum!
And as a cygnet

stranded by a river
keeps rasping its calls to the father it loves
trapped and lifeless in treacherous mesh,
so I keep crying, crying out to you,
     poor Father,   160

caught by surprise as you bathed, your body
now cold within death's earthen bed.
     And my cries find no rest.
Sharp the axe-blade that cut you, and sharp,
Father, the schemes that were laid
while you journeyed from Troy.
Your welcome home, no laurels,
no crown, but a sword's double edge
and your wife designing the crime
that she helped Aigisthos commit   170
     so he'd lie in her bed.

The CHORUS *enters singing and dancing joyfully.*

CHORUS (*severally*) —Daughter of Agamemnon,
Electra, I've run all the way
to your home in the wild hills.

—A man came, a man who drinks milk for wine
came with his herd through these mountains.

—He tells of a proclamation.

—Three days from now, the festal sacrifice
at Hera's temple.

     —All would-be brides   180
are asked to celebrate her holy rites.

ELECTRA (*singing*) No longer, my friends, do I go forth
lighthearted, dressed in gleaming robes
and necklaces of gold.
In my sorrow I cannot lead

the songs of your bridal choir
nor step with you lightly in circling dance.
In tears I spend my nights.
Day after day the tears
come streaming from swollen eyes.   190
Look at me—raw stubble on my head,
my robe more holes than cloth.
Are such things fit for Agamemnon's
royal daughter? Fit for my father
whom Troy remembers well
as the man who brought her low?

CHORUS (*severally*) —The goddess works wonders. Come.

    —Borrow the fine things you need. Please
    let me lend you a soft cloak.

    —A robe.   200

            —Gold to make everything gleam.

    —Your tears do not honor the gods.
    Do you think that tears can defeat
    your enemies?

            —Worship the gods
    with prayers, not wails, and then
    you shall know brighter days.

ELECTRA No god gives heed to my battle cries.
Heaven disdains me and has long forgot
my father's sacrifice,   210
though I wail for the dead and wail
for one alive, the wanderer
who somewhere in a strange land
discovers warmth and rest
only at peasants' fires—
and he the son of a far-famed king.
And I must live in a poor man's house,
my spirit wearing thin,
exiled from home and heritage

to mountain crags while my mother
settles a new mate
in her murder-bloodied bed.

220

CHORUSLEADER (*speaking*)
For bringing evil days to Greece and to your house,
your mother's sister Helen bears the blame.

ELECTRA (speaking)
Oh look! No time for more tears.
Women, look—strangers near the house,
men ready for ambush. Quick!
Run down that path. I'll slip inside.
Give them no chance to rob or rape us.

ORESTES, PYLADES, *and their attendants emerge from
hiding.*

ELECTRA *freezes at the strangers' approach while the*
CHORUS *retreats and stops, watching.*

ORESTES Stay. Don't be afraid of me.

230

ELECTRA Apollo, don't let me die!

ORESTES I'd rather kill someone I hate.

ORESTES *reaches toward* ELECTRA *but does not touch
her.*

ELECTRA (*flinching*) Go! Don't paw. No need to paw me.

ORESTES I have just reason to touch you.

ELECTRA Why lurk in ambush with a sword?

ORESTES Stay. You won't regret it.

ELECTRA I have no choice. You're stronger than I.

ORESTES I come with a message from your brother.

ELECTRA Then you *are* a friend. Is he alive or dead?

ORESTES Alive. I want to tell you good news first.   240

ELECTRA The best of news! Heaven bless you.

ORESTES I give the blessing back. We both share it.

ELECTRA My fugitive brother—where is he now?

ORESTES No law, no city steadies him. He drifts.

ELECTRA Not lacking, surely, for life's daily needs?

ORESTES No, but a fugitive is powerless.

ELECTRA Do you come here at his orders?

ORESTES Yes, to learn if you're alive. Then, where you live,
                                             and how.

ELECTRA Look first at my wasted flesh.

ORESTES Drawn so thin I pity you.   250

ELECTRA And my head, my ugly hacked-off hair.

ORESTES Brother and dead father—you're twice hurt by grief.

ELECTRA These two—what else could be more loved?

ORESTES Oh, what do you think your brother feels for you?

ELECTRA He's far away but close to my heart.

ORESTES (*gesturing toward the farmhouse*)
        Why live there, remote from town?

29

ELECTRA Stranger, I was given in a marriage that may be my death.

ORESTES I know your brother grieves. To someone highborn?

ELECTRA No, though my father intended otherwise.

ORESTES Explain so your brother will understand.   260

ELECTRA I live in my husband's isolated house.

ORESTES The house of a herdsman or dirt farmer.

ELECTRA He's poor but noble in mind. He treats me reverently.

ORESTES Reverence? How does your husband show it?

ELECTRA Never—not once—has he dared touch my bed.

ORESTES Chaste because of holy vows or from disdain?

ELECTRA He thought he should not so insult my lineage.

ORESTES But wasn't he pleased to take you in marriage?

ELECTRA Stranger, the man who gave me to him has no right.

ORESTES Only Orestes has that right. He could be vengeful.   270

ELECTRA Fearfully so. But self-control runs in my husband's grain.

ORESTES I see.
        Noble, as you said. One should do something for him.

ELECTRA My brother will—once he comes home.

ORESTES And your mother is content with your way of life?

ELECTRA Stranger, women love their men, not their children.

ORESTES But why should Aigisthos so insult you?

ELECTRA Because children born of this marriage would be powerless.

ORESTES Because—indeed!—such children would not seek ven-
                                                    geance?

ELECTRA His very scheme. May he pay me a just price.   280

ORESTES Does he know you're still virgin?

ELECTRA He does not know. We've kept our silence.

ORESTES (*indicating the* CHORUS)
          Are they your friends, these women with open ears?

ELECTRA Friends, oh yes, who keep their lips closed.

ORESTES What should Orestes do *if* he comes home?

ELECTRA You ask this? He must come! It's time to act.

ORESTES *When* he comes, then, how might he kill your father's
                                                    murderers?

ELECTRA Daring against them what they dared against my father.

ORESTES And with his help would you dare kill your mother?

ELECTRA Yes! And with the same axe that destroyed my father.   290

ORESTES Do I tell him this? Will you stand firm?

ELECTRA I'd die to let blood from my mother's throat.

ORESTES Fierce!
          If only Orestes could hear you.

ELECTRA Stranger, I wouldn't recognize him.

31

ORESTES No wonder—separated when you were young.

ELECTRA Only one of my friends would know him.

ORESTES The one who concealed him to prevent his murder?

ELECTRA Yes, my father's tutor, an old man now.

ORESTES Was your father's body granted a decent tomb?   300

ELECTRA Granted as he was granted expulsion from his own house.

ORESTES Harsh words. My god, how just hearing of miseries
         endured by others can sink sharp teeth into a man.
         But tell me more so I may bring your brother
         the news, however joyless, that he needs to hear.
         Pity, impossible for lowborn brutes, comes
         only to those who inherit noble feelings.
         But even they pay dearly to scruple overmuch.

CHORUSLEADER My heart has the same urge.
             Far from the troubles of the city and her people,   310
             I know nothing. But I want to learn.

ELECTRA If talk is needed, I will tell you as a friend
         how heavy fortune has weighed on me and my father.
         But now that you force my words, I beg you, stranger,
         tell Orestes of the wrongs done both of us,
         that I wear robes fit for a cowshed
         and bend beneath filth and under a roof like this
         spend my days—I who came from a royal house—
         I, callusing my fingers at the loom to weave cloth
         so that my naked body has some shred to wear;   320
         I, bowed by the weight of water on my head.
         Without one holiday to lead these girls in dance,
         yet must I shun other wives because I am virgin
         and stand ashamed before Castor, now one of the gods,
         whom I was meant to marry, my kin, my own kind.
         Meanwhile, my mother in Oriental luxury

lolls on the throne waited on by Asian
slaves my father took as spoils of war.
They wear vests of fine soft wool fastened by gold.
My father's blood has gone black, still rotting   330
beneath that roof, while the man who killed him
exults, careering headlong in the chariot
my father drove, and clutches in his murderous hand
the scepter once wielded to command the Greeks.
And Agamemnon's tomb—no honor paid,
not one libation, no myrtle sprig,
the altar bare of any ornament.
Sodden with strong drink, my mother's husband—
the Glorious they call him—staggers on the grave
and flings rocks at my father's memorial stone   340
and rants against us with a reckless mouth:
"Where *is* Orestes? Where? How well your son's presence
guards your tomb." Thus does he mock my absent brother.

But, stranger, I beg you, tell him this, too.
Each part of me sends him its message,
hands and tongue and spirit in distress,
my cropped head, my grief for the one who fathered him.
Shameful if the son whose father leveled Troy
cannot himself kill one lone man.
But my brother is young and strong and nobly born.   350

                              The FARMER *enters.*

CHORUSLEADER Electra, look there—at your husband, I mean.
               He's left the fields. He's on his way home.

     FARMER (*to* ELECTRA) Well! Who are these strangers at my door?
               Why come to the gates of this farm? What
               do they want from me? Shameful—and you know it—
               for women to dally in the company of young men.

    ELECTRA My dear, don't put me under suspicion
               before you know the facts. The strangers came
               bringing me news of Orestes.

(*to* ORESTES *and* PYLADES)

Strangers, forgive his outburst.   360

FARMER What do they say? He's alive?

ELECTRA Alive, so they tell me. They seem worth trusting.

FARMER Does he remember the wrongs done you and your father?

ELECTRA I hope so, but a fugitive is powerless.

FARMER What do they tell you about Orestes?

ELECTRA He sent them to observe firsthand the wrongs done me.

FARMER Aren't some plain to see? And you've told them all the rest?

ELECTRA They know everything. Nothing was held back.

FARMER Shouldn't our doors have been opened long before now?

(*to* ORESTES *and* PYLADES)

Please come inside. In trade for good news   370
you'll find the food and drink my house
stores for its guests.

(*to the attendants, who obey*)

[Take in their gear.]

(*to* ORESTES *and* PYLADES)

And don't refuse me. Sent by a friend, you come here
as my friends. Though I must live by my sweat,
I'll never show myself ill-bred in manners.

ORESTES (*to* ELECTRA) My god, is this the man who does not
consummate your marriage lest he shame Orestes?

ELECTRA He is called poor Electra's husband.

ORESTES So!   380
           There's no precise mark for recognizing worth.
           Appearances confuse. I have seen the son
           of a noble father existing as a nothing,
           and able children born of bad stock,
           and famine in a rich man's spirit,
           and fine conscience in a poor man's frame.

           How does one find the right criterion?
           Wealth? But that's a sorry test.
           Lack of property? But being without brings
           madness; sheer need turns man into monster.   390
           Shall I consider arms? What soldier confronting
           a spear thinks it indicates the spearman's courage?
           But enough of such speculation.

           Witness this man, not great among his countrymen,
           not puffed up by his family's rank. He's one of the crowd,
           but I find him a natural aristocrat.
           Isn't it senseless to be led astray
           by preconceived notions and not judge good breeding
           by a man's company and his manners?

           [Such people bring credit to city   400
           and family. But flesh empty of purpose
           is a statue set to decorate a public square.
           Nor does holding a spear distinguish strength from weakness.
           Only character matters, and courage.]

           But, for Agamemnon's deserving son
           who is not here, yet here through me, we accept
           your hospitality.

                                   (to the attendants, who obey)

                           Forward now, it's your duty,
           into the house.

(*to* ELECTRA)

            Better a poor man who's willing   410
than a rich man as my host.
I have only praise for the welcome found here.
Still, I could wish your brother knew good fortune
and were now leading me into a house more fortunate.
As I come, so may he. Though human prophecies
may be dismissed, Apollo's oracle speaks true.

        ORESTES *and* PYLADES *exeunt into the farmhouse.*

CHORUSLEADER Now, Electra, as not before, joy
        lights my heart. Fortune, slow in her coming,
        may take a stand here for the best.

    ELECTRA (*to the* FARMER)
        You reckless man, you know the house lacks everything.   420
        Why receive guests who far outrank you?

    FARMER Why not? If they are noble—as they seem, won't they
        be satisfied by any food, plain or fancy?

    ELECTRA Because you lead a plain life, you miss the point.
        Go to the old man who brought up my father.
        He's banished from the city. You'll find him
        herding his flocks near the river
        that marks the boundary between Argos and Sparta.
        Give him my order that he come to your house
        bringing food to entertain our guests.   430
        He will be pleased, oh yes! He'll thank the gods
        to hear the boy whose life he saved is living still.
        My mother, as you know, would give us nothing
        from my father's house, and bitterness would fill her
        brimming over should she learn Orestes lives.

    FARMER Then, as you wish, I'll take the message to the old man.
        Best hurry to the house and tidy it, begin

your preparations. Improvise. We have much
a woman needs to fix a hearty meal.
I'm sure the house stores forage enough   440
to fill their bellies for at least one day.
But whenever I give such matters any thought,
I think that money grants a man power
to treat guests handsomely and preserve his own body
when he gets sick. But a day's worth of forage
costs little. Rich or poor, a man can eat
only so much before he's satisfied.

> The FARMER *exits to fetch the* OLD MAN.

> ELECTRA *exits into the farmhouse.*

CHORUS (*singing and dancing*)
    Once, the famed ships sailed eager toward Troy,
    oars beyond count pushing them onward
    escorted by Sea-Nymphs dancing their songs,   450
    and a dolphin loving the flutes
    leaped and rolled round and around
    the dark beaks of prows
    while decks echoed under the unresting strides
    of Achilles, Thetis' son,
    who, with Agamemnon, surged to Troy,
    that fortress rising where its river meets the sea,

    and Sea-Nymphs leaving their sheltered coves
    carried the burden Hephaistos forged
    on his loud-ringing anvil—arms wrought of gold—   460
    up over Pelion's cliffs,
    up holy Mount Ossa where the Nymphs
    made search from high crags
    for the boy whom the Centaur-father brought
    into manhood, Thetis' son,
    the sea-child born with quick strides to be
    a light for Atreus' sons and all of Greece.

    And I heard in Nauplia's harbor
    from someone who'd fled out of Troy

a firsthand account, Achilles,   470
of your famous shield, its pulsing designs—
gold come alive!—wrought to bring Trojans
down to their knees in fear,
and quick on the roundshield's rim
Perseus the throat-cutter
flying on winged heels above churning seas
brandishes the Gorgon's head
in the presence of Maia's son,
country-bred Hermes,
the messenger of Zeus himself,   480

and wheeling in shield's very center
the sun drawn by wingèd horses
blazes out noon's white-hot light
and stars in bright chorus hum as they whirl—
Pleiades, Hyades, frightening fires
too bright for Hector's eyes,
and crouched in the helmet's gold
Sphinxes work talons
deep into prey lured close by their crooning,
and on the body-armor, flames   490
roar on the Chimera's breath
and her claws harrow earth
as she runs from Pegasus' flying hooves,

and around the murderous sword-blade, war-stallions
gallop, their hooves raising clouds of black dust.
The commander of spear-hurling Greeks—

(*turning, addressing the absent* CLYTEMNESTRA)

you killed him—you, his wife,
Tyndareos' daughter, driven by malice.
For that the gods in heaven
will send you to your death.   500
And may I see your throat beneath the knife.
And may I see your life's blood pumping out.

The OLD MAN *enters carrying a lamb and other gifts.*

OLD MAN (*speaking*)
Where can she be? Where's the young lady I've served—
Agamemnon's child? I brought her up.
How steep the path to her house—
no easy going for a wrinkled old man.
No matter. To reach a friend I won't be
hindered by my hunched back and these shaky knees.

ELECTRA, *hearing him, enters from the farmhouse.*

My daughter, here you are!
See what I've brought you from my flock—   510
a lamb that was still on the teat, and here,
crowns of flowers, and cheeses fresh from my press,
and this treasure from Dionysos, not much
but aged well, has a fine bouquet, enough
to make a sweet cup when it's mixed with weaker wine.
Have someone take these inside for your guests.
And here I stand in worn-out robes
wanting to wipe the tears from my eyes.

ELECTRA   Old man, why are you crying? Do you still,
after all this time, remember my troubles?   520
Or do you mourn Orestes, a helpless fugitive,
and mourn my father? You held him when he was a baby,
taught him as he grew—and for what?

OLD MAN   For nothing. But this is what I really could not bear—
his lonely tomb. On my way to you, I stopped there
to prostrate myself and weep. No one saw me.
I loosened the wineskin brought for your guests and poured
a hasty libation. Then I put myrtle around the tomb.
And there on the altar I saw black fleece,
a sheep sacrificed, its blood still fresh,   530
and a curl of chestnut hair cut from someone's head.
Child, I wonder at such recklessness.
No Argive dares approach that tomb.

But someone came in stealth—perhaps your brother,
home and shocked by a father's neglected grave.
Go there. Inspect the curl. Compare it with your own
cropped hair. See if the colors match.
There's often a natural resemblance
in children of the same father's blood.

ELECTRA It does not become an old man wise as you to joke,   540
suggesting that my courageous brother would crawl here
in secret because he fears Aigisthos.
And that snip of hair—how can it match mine?
Cut for the wrestling school, a man's hair grows out coarse;
combing keeps a woman's soft and fine. No comparison!
Old man, many have hair of the same texture,
same color, yet share no drop of common blood.

OLD MAN Yes but, child, go see the bootprints on the path.
Perhaps those feet and yours measure out alike.

ELECTRA Now how can a footprint be made on stony ground?   550
But if such prints exist, a sister's foot is
not equal to her brother's, nor a woman's
to that of a man. Male feet grow bigger.

OLD MAN Is there not—supposing your brother *has* come home—
a piece of your weaving you'd know him by,
something he wore when he was smuggled from his death?

ELECTRA Don't you recall how young I was when Orestes
was taken away? Supposing I *had* made clothing
that fit him as a child, could he wear it now?
Or did the cloth grow along with his body?   560
No! At the tomb some stranger, struck by pity,
cut his hair, or some native outwitting the spies.

OLD MAN Strangers—where are your guests? I'd like
to see them, ask them about your brother.

ELECTRA Just leaving the house to come our way.

ORESTES and PYLADES *enter from the farmhouse.*

OLD MAN Wellborn, I'd say, but first impressions don't always
ring true. Many a wellborn man is worthless.
No matter. I'll pay my respects to your guest.

ORESTES Sir, my respects.

(*to* ELECTRA)

To which of your friends, Electra,   570
does this ancient remnant of a man belong?

ELECTRA Stranger, he brought up my father.

ORESTES What! Is he the man who smuggled out your brother?

ELECTRA The very man who saved his life—if he still lives.

ORESTES Oh!
Why does he squint at me as if examining
a bright new silver coin? Do I look like someone he knows?

ELECTRA Perhaps in you he sees Orestes. You're the same age.

ORESTES He was fond of Orestes. But why is he shuffling around
me?

ELECTRA Stranger, I don't know. He surprises me.   580

OLD MAN My lady, pray! Daughter, pray to the gods!

ELECTRA Pray for what? Something absent, something here?

OLD MAN God makes treasured hope come true. Reach! Hold it fast!

ELECTRA Gods in heaven! What are you saying, old man?

OLD MAN Child, look at the one you love best.

41

ELECTRA Are you so old you've lost your good sense?

ONL MAN Lost my good sense, have I, telling you your brother—

ELECTRA What do you mean? Old man, I can't hope for such news.

OLD MAN —Orestes, Agamemnon's son, stands here before my eyes?

ELECTRA Convince me. By what mark should I know him?   590

OLD MAN The scar over his eyebrow. He got it by tumbling—
remember?—when he chased with you after a fawn.

ELECTRA With me? Yes, I do see the cut—long healed.

OLD MAN Then why hold back? The brother you love—embrace
                                                     him!

ELECTRA No more delay. Dear man, your evidence
persuades my heart.

                              (*embracing* ORESTES)

                    At last, you—here, real!
     I'd lost all hope.

ORESTES   And I hold you at last.

ELECTRA I never thought it possible.   600

ORESTES   Nor did I hope.

ELECTRA You *are* he?

ORESTES   Yes, your one and only ally.
     I look for a net to land our catch,
     and it *shall* be found. Else, why believe in gods
     if wrong is not punished but rewarded?

CHORUS (*singing and dancing*) You come, come at last,
          O day we were helpless to speed.

42

You dawn with new light. You blaze on the city
signaling one whose long-ago flight   610
sent him homeless, defeated, to spend the slow years
wandering in exile.
Now, our time has come. A god, friends, a god
brings victory to us.
Raise your hands high,
        raise voices high,
                send prayers to the gods
that by some fortune that conquers misfortune
your brother will enter the city in triumph.

ORESTES (*speaking*)
        May that day come. This day I know the sweetness   620
        of my sister's arms. And we'll embrace again, later.
        And you, old man, you've come at the right time
        to tell me how I repay my father's murderer
        and my mother, his partner, his unhallowed wife.
        Do I have one friend who wishes me well?
        Or has misfortune made me bankrupt of friends?
        With whom can I join? By night or by day?
        What road can I take against my enemies?

OLD MAN Child, misfortune leaves you no friends.
        It's rare good luck, I'll tell you, to find   630
        anyone who stands by through good times and bad.
        But you—completely stripped of friends,
        no hope of friendship left—come, listen to me.
        In your hands you hold all the fortune you need
        to repossess your heritage and your people.

ORESTES And how may we accomplish this?

OLD MAN By killing Thyestes' son and your mother.

ORESTES I've come for just this crown. But how do I win it?

OLD MAN You won't if you enter the city.

ORESTES Defended by a well-armed garrison?   640

OLD MAN Of course. He fears you. He gets little sleep.

ORESTES So. Tell me how to proceed.

OLD MAN I just now thought of something. Listen to this.

ORESTES Go ahead. I'll listen if it's worthwhile.

OLD MAN Aigisthos—I saw him as I came here.

ORESTES You have my attention. Where?

OLD MAN (*gesturing*) Over in the meadows where his horses graze.

ORESTES Doing what? I begin to see hope.

OLD MAN Preparing a feast, I think, for the Nymphs.

ORESTES In thanks for living children or one not yet born?   650

OLD MAN I know only that he was making ready for sacrifice.

ORESTES Were free men there? Or was he alone with his slaves?

OLD MAN No citizens, just his household staff.

ORESTES Is anyone there who'd recognize me?

OLD MAN No, only slaves who never saw you as a boy.

ORESTES If I win, will they give me allegiance?

OLD MAN Slaves know who's master. That's to your advantage.

ORESTES How—and when—may I edge close to him?

OLD MAN Go where he'll see you when he makes the sacrifice.

ORESTES The road, then, skirts the meadow?   660

OLD MAN Yes. He'll see you there and invite you to the feast.

ORESTES If god so wishes, he'll find his share tastes bitter.

OLD MAN Then, as the dice fall, make your next play.

ORESTES Good advice. And where is my mother?

OLD MAN In town, but she'll join her husband for the feast.

ORESTES Why did she not go with him?

OLD MAN She trembles at the blame on people's tongues.

ORESTES Yes, she must know the whole nation accuses her.

OLD MAN Exactly. They hate that ungodly woman.

ORESTES How do I kill them both?   670

ELECTRA I myself will arrange my mother's death.

ORESTES And fortune will neatly dispose of him.

ELECTRA (*indicating the* OLD MAN)
Let him serve both of us in this.

ORESTES As you wish. How will you seek our mother's death?

ELECTRA (*to the* OLD MAN) Go to Clytemnestra, old friend.
Announce that Electra has borne a male child.

OLD MAN Some time ago or recently?

ELECTRA Ten days ago. It's time for the postpartum rites.

OLD MAN Does this have bearing on your mother's death?

ELECTRA My mother shall come when she hears I've borne a son. 680

OLD MAN But why, my child, would she concern herself with you?

ELECTRA She'll come. She'll weep about my son's high rank.

OLD MAN Perhaps. But what are you really saying?

ELECTRA When my mother comes, she shall be killed.

OLD MAN Oh! Let her enter these gates, then.

ELECTRA And won't she find she's at the gates of death?

OLD MAN If only I might see this before I die!

ELECTRA (*indicating* ORESTES) Take him now to the right place.

OLD MAN Where Aigisthos prepares for sacrifice?

ELECTRA When you meet my mother, give her my message. 690

OLD MAN As if you'd spoken it yourself.

ELECTRA (*to* ORESTES) You have your task: take first turn at killing.

ORESTES As soon as my guide points the way.

OLD MAN I'm more than willing to escort you.

> ORESTES, ELECTRA, *and the* OLD MAN *pray.*

ORESTES O Zeus of our Fathers, be Router of enemies.

ELECTRA And pity us, for we have suffered pitifully.

OLD MAN Have pity on those who sprang from your seed.

ELECTRA And Hera whose power kindles flames on our altars,

ORESTES give us victory if you find justice in our prayer.

OLD MAN Give it for him they justly avenge.   700

ORESTES I call to your earthen house, Father godlessly murdered.

ELECTRA (*kneeling and beating on the ground*)
Earth, holy queen, I give you these hands that would
wake him.

OLD MAN Wake, wake to defend the children you love.

ELECTRA (*rising*) Now rise, bring the legions of dead as our allies,

ORESTES the dead you commanded whose spears brought Troy ruin,

OLD MAN who hate those defiled by ungodly crimes.

The prayer ends.

ORESTES You, forever wronged by our mother, can you hear?

OLD MAN I'm sure your father hears your prayers. Our time draws near.

ELECTRA Yes, quite sure.

(*to* ORESTES)

Be the man you need to be.   710
[It cannot be put too strongly: Aigisthos must die.
If *you* fall losing the contest and your life,
I, too, would die. No, don't tell me I'd be saved.
My hand would drive a sword right through my heart.
No matter what happens, I shall be ready.]
If news should come that fortune favors you,
victory cries will ring through the house. But if you die—
silence, absolute. That's all I need tell you.

(*to the* CHORUS)

Women, do this for me: at contest's end, let voices
blaze to signal the outcome. I shall be waiting,   720
my arm raised and ready to plunge home the sword.
No enemy of mine will ever celebrate
his victory by raping me.

ELECTRA *exits into the farmhouse. The* OLD MAN *exits,*
followed by ORESTES, PYLADES, *and their attendants.*

CHORUS (*singing and dancing*)
How tender the lamb as it suckled its mother!
Now only old men know stories of Pan
but this tale still rings through the wild hills.
Listen—the pipes breathe a reedy
sweetness! Pan the divine shepherd
plays to his flock as he lifts up
the lamb—grown, fleeced with fine gold—   730
and carries it off. From a high, rocky
ledge, a herald shouts to the valley:
"Assemble, assemble, nobles
of Argos! Heaven sends a portent
to make you shiver.
It confirms your king." And people danced the hymns
acclaiming Atreus.

The gods' golden hearths opened wide, and all,
all the town was alight as fire
on every altar rose to a bright blaze.   740
And listen—the Muses' servant,
a flute, lifts its clear, lovely trill.
And songs of the golden ram lit
sweet desires. Then Thyestes
played his trick. He lured his brother's
wife into his bed and in the heat
of secret love persuaded her
to steal the ram from Atreus.
And he howled to the people:
"*I* am your king, for I have in *my* keeping   750
the ram with the golden fleece."

Then thunder boomed, then Zeus
reversed the stars' radiant sweep
and the dazzling sunlight
and morning's white face, and the sun
for the first time drove up in the west
while lightning flamed and seared earth,
but storm clouds flew north, hoarding
their rain, and robbed of sweet water,
the green oases, even that of Libyan Zeus,   760
became lifeless desert.

I cannot know the truth
of this tale, but the reason, they say,
the sun's golden face changed its course
and brought such misfortune to men
was heavenly judgment pronounced
against crimes that mortals commit.
And stories that strike fear in mankind
remind us to worship the gods.
But you, sister of famous brothers—you forgot.   770
You murdered your husband.

Offstage cries are heard.

CHORUSLEADER (*speaking*) EA! EA!
Do you hear the howls? Do I imagine them—
shouts like an earthquake's thunder?
Sounds ride on the wind.
My lady! Electra! Come out, come out!

ELECTRA *runs, sword in hand, from the farmhouse.*

ELECTRA What's happening? The contest is over?

CHORUSLEADER I don't know. I heard the howls of death.

ELECTRA I heard them, too. They came from far away.

CHORUSLEADER Far away, yes, but plain to hear.   780

49

ELECTRA Did an enemy howl, or a friend?

CHORUSLEADER I don't know. Such a muddle of cries!

ELECTRA They plunge the sword in my heart. Why wait?

CHORUSLEADER Stop! Wait till you know what fortune brings.

ELECTRA No. We're beaten. Otherwise, wouldn't there be some news?

CHORUSLEADER News will come. It's no small matter to kill a king.

The MESSENGER *enters.*

MESSENGER Now let winning light up your faces.
I bring you word that Orestes has won.
Agamemnon's murderer Aigisthos
sprawls on the ground. Give thanks to the gods.   790

ELECTRA Who are you? How can you make me believe you?

MESSENGER Don't you know your brother's servant?

ELECTRA Welcome! all I could see was my own fear.
Now I recognize you.
My father's murderer is truly dead?

MESSENGER He's dead. So you'll believe me, I repeat it.

ELECTRA O gods, O Justice, you watched and waited.
At last you come.

(*to the* MESSENGER)

How *did* Aigisthos die?
What weapon, what kind of wound?   800

MESSENGER Soon after leaving your house, we marched
on a road built wide enough for two chariots abreast

till we found the new lord of Argos.
He was walking through a stream-watered garden
picking fresh myrtle to wreathe his head.
He sees us and calls, "Hello, strangers. Who are you?
Where are you going? What is your country?"
Orestes calls back, "Thessalians. Heading
for the river at Olympia and a sacrifice to Zeus."
Hearing that, Aigisthos says,   810
"Now you must be my guests and join me in the feast.
It happens I'm sacrificing a calf
to the Nymphs. Put off your journey till dawn—
delay makes no difference—and enter my house."
As he speaks, he takes our hands
tugging us forward. "You must not say No."
And when we're inside, he orders a slave
to fetch water quickly so that his guests
may stand at the altar with clean hands.
But Orestes tells him, "We have already bathed   820
in living water to make ourselves pure for the gods.
If you insist that strangers share the rites with citizens,
we are ready, my lord. We shall not refuse."

All conversation ended then.
The slaves guarding that high and mighty master
laid down their spears and put their hands to work.
Some carried bowls outside to catch the victim's blood,
some brought baskets, others built the fire and set cauldrons
straight around the altar-hearth. Their noise filled the house.
And taking barley grains, your mother's husband   830
cast them on the altar as he prayed:
"Nymphs who hallow these rocks, again I honor you
with sacrifice so that my wife and I shall prosper
as we do now, and that my enemies, as now, will fail."
Enemies—you and Orestes! But my own lord
prayed without a sound for something else—
to seize his home and heritage.
                              Aigisthos took
the ritual knife from its basket, cut the calf's forelock
and placed it with his right hand on the sacred fire,   840

51

and then, the calf on a slave's shoulders, its neck pulled back,
he cuts its throat and says this to your brother,
"Thessalians claim the skills of gentlemen—how neatly
they can dismember a bull, how quickly
break the wildest horse. My guest, the sword is yours.
Show me the substance behind Thessalian talk."

Orestes takes up a newly sharpened blade,
flings back his cloak to free his arms for work,
dismisses the waiting slaves, and chooses
Pylades as acolyte. Taking the calf   850
by a hoof, he lays the white flesh bare.
Groin to throat and back again, he stripped off the hide
faster than a runner can round two laps,
and he slit the belly open. Then Aigisthos
took the innards to read what they foretold.
Part of the liver was missing; portal vein
and gall bladder both had an ominous look.
Aigisthos grows rigid, and my lord asks,
"Why so dispirited?"
                              "Stranger, treachery   860
stalks me from abroad by the man I most hate,
Agamemnon's son, the kingdom's enemy and mine."
And Orestes replies, "Can a king fear
a fugitive? No, it's time to feast.
Let someone take this knife and bring me
a cleaver. I'll break the rib cage."
And he cracks the bone. Aigisthos wanted
to inspect the heart and lungs. As he stooped low,
your brother, rising to his fullest height,
drove the cleaver in Aigisthos' neck and split   870
his backbone. And his whole body thrashed, up, down,
flung by convulsions. He died hard.
The slaves, wide-eyed, grabbed up their spears,
many to battle a mere two. But sheer gut-courage
let Pylades and Orestes stand firm, weapons
ready. Then Orestes says, "I come here
bent on no harm to the state or those who follow me.
I, Orestes, have avenged my father's

murder. Long ago you served him faithfully.
No need to kill his son."   880
                              When they heard that,
they lowered their spears, and he was recognized
by one old man who'd long served the court.
Right there, cheering him, crying in triumph,
they put a crown on your brother's head. And he comes
bringing you a head—not the Gorgon's
but his whom you hate, Aigisthos. Yes, blood for blood,
his bitter loan came due. He paid with death.

                              The MESSENGER *exits.*

CHORUS (*singing and dancing*)
          Dance with us, dance, O Electra, step light.
          Bound like a fawn   890
          soaring toward heaven, shining with joy.
          He wins a crown
          finer by far than Olympia's prize.
          Your brother wins! Come
                    weave, as I dance,
                              your garlands of victory song.

ELECTRA (*speaking*) O light! O sun wheeling brilliant above me!
          O Earth and Night whose darkness was all I saw,
          now my eyes are open and free—
          my father's murderer lies on the ground.   900
          I must find, bring out whatever ribbons, beads
          the house still holds to grace a head,
          to crown my brother who brings victory home.

                    ELECTRA *exits into the farmhouse.*

          ORESTES, PYLADES, *and their attendants enter carrying*
                              Aigisthos' body and head.

CHORUS (*singing and dancing*)
          Make him a wreath that could grace a god's head.
          Our voices will dance,
          our dancing feet echo heaven's delight.

A king we may love
because of his just rule shall rule us again.
Injustice lies dead! Come
    sing the sweet music,   910
        cry out *joy, joy, he has won!*

ELECTRA, *carrying two wreaths, enters from the*
farmhouse.

ELECTRA (*crowning* ORESTES *as she speaks*)
Victory becomes a son whose father
battled Troy and brought home victory. Orestes,
accept these braided ribbons as your crown,
for you return not from running some bloodless
footrace but from killing the enemy,
Aigisthos, who destroyed your father and mine.

(*crowning* PYLADES)

And you, obedient to the lessons of your most
pious father—you fought beside him. Pylades,
accept this crown, for you shared in the contest   920
equally. Always may I see you fortune-blessed.

ORESTES The gods, Electra—think first of them as the cause
of our good fortune. Then, only then, praise me,
mere servant to fortune and the gods.
Let deeds, not words, tell you of Aigisthos'
killing. Nothing proves it more clearly
than what we deliver.

(*holding up Aigisthos' head*)

I give you his head.
Do as you wish—toss it to the dogs, set it out
as carrion for the air's children,   930
impale it on a stake. Now the man
once called your lord and master is your slave.

ELECTRA Shame calls for silence, but I long to speak out.

ORESTES Why not? Now you have nothing to fear.

ELECTRA Except censure for speaking ill of the dead.

ORESTES No one would blame you.

ELECTRA Our city is squeamish. It dotes on casting blame.

ORESTES My sister, speak as you will, for you and I, both
hating him implacably, have done this together.

ORESTES *hands Aigisthos' head to* ELECTRA.

ELECTRA (*holding and addressing the head*) So be it.   940
Where to begin to catalogue your wrongs?
Where end? And how fill in the parts between?
Each day before dawn I never once stopped
rehearsing what I would have told you to your face
if only I'd been free from fear that lasted
much too long. Now we *are* free. And I present you
with the words that should have reached your living ears.

(*putting down the head so that it faces her*)

You ruined me, for no just reason orphaned
my brother and me of the father we loved.
And you shamed yourself, killing my mother's husband   950
who led the Greeks to Troy while you—you shirked the war.
You came to such a point of stupid brutishness
that you dared hope, after fouling my father's bed,
that my mother would prove a virtuous woman.
But he who beds another's wife in secret
should be aware, when marriage springs its trap,
that she shall not restore for him
the chastity she has already flouted.
Your life spread pain, though you thought it hurt no one.
You saw the shamefulness of godless marriage, yes,   960

55

and knew my mother had wed an impious man.
But both of you were tainted then—you shouldering
her destiny and she, your wickedness.
You must have heard the talk that buzzed through Argos:
"Oh look. He lets her have her way in everything."

Sheer disgrace—to see not husband but wife
dominate a household! And this I also find
abhorrent—male children called in public
not by their father's name but by the mother's.
The man who marries to advance himself remains   970
a nothing, for his wife still has the final word.
You didn't know that fact. Ignorance fooled you
into boasting of the power great wealth gave you.
It's no more than a fleeting companion.
Only human character stands firm
and lasts forever, surmounting every trouble,
while wealth unjustly gained by public mischief
flowers for a short time, then takes wing.

And your way with women—too crass for innocent
lips. I'll merely hint at what I know.   980
How you strutted and preened, living in a king's house,
showing off your well-made body. But I want no
girl-faced husband. Give me a man,
for *his* sons make courageous soldiers
while pretty boys can only decorate the dance.

(*taking up Aigisthos' head and pitching it toward his
                                                  body*)

Be damned! I regret you cannot know how you have
paid at last a just price. You who work evil
may start the race on a sure foot, but never think
you've outrun justice and won before the final turn
is rounded and you sprint down life's last lap.   990

CHORUSLEADER   The dreadful things he did call for the dreadful
               death you gave him. Justice has great strength.

ELECTRA   Strength indeed. Now to dispose of the body, consign it
to the dark so that my mother, when she comes
for sacrifice, does not see the corpse.

ORESTES' *attendants, carrying Aigisthos' remains, exeunt
into the farmhouse.*

ELECTRA *turns to follow them.*

ORESTES   Stop! Enough! We need to talk more.

ELECTRA   About what? Are soldiers coming to help him?

ORESTES   Not soldiers, but the mother who gave me birth.

ELECTRA   She's carried to our net, then, in glittering style—
riding in a chariot, wearing splendid robes of state.   1000

ORESTES   What shall we do? Kill our own mother?

ELECTRA   Now that you see her, do you feel pity?

ORESTES   Pity—
she brought me up, she bore me. How can I kill her?

ELECTRA   The way she slaughtered your father and mine.

ORESTES   Phoibos, your oracle was brutal!

ELECTRA   If even Apollo's judgment fails, is anyone wise?

ORESTES   Kill my mother—his voice should not have told me that.

ELECTRA   How can it harm you to avenge our father?

ORESTES   For killing her, I'll stand trial—I, pure till then.   1010

ELECTRA   Not honoring a father—that's sacrilege!

ORESTES I know. But my mother's murder—how must I pay?

ELECTRA Would you choose someone else to avenge *your* father?

ORESTES God, did some demon of vengeance speak in your voice?

ELECTRA At Delphi? From the sacred tripod? No.

ORESTES I'll never believe the prophecy rings true.

ELECTRA Let no coward's thoughts topple your manhood,
but bring to this task the same guile our mother used
to kill her lord and husband with Aigisthos' help.

ORESTES It shall be done. I start on a course I dread.   1020
I'll do things I dread. If that please the gods,
so be it. For me this sport is bitter, not sweet.

ORESTES *exits into the farmhouse.*

CLYTEMNESTRA, *accompanied by her Trojan slave-
women, enters in a regally caparisoned horse-drawn
wagon.*

CHORUS (*severally*)—My lady, queen of Argos.

—Daughter of Tyndareos.

—Sister of Zeus' sons, Castor and Polydeukes,
twin stars lighting a new blaze in heaven
and honored as saviors of men
who sail the storm-tossed waves.

—You merit reverence for equaling
The gods themselves in wealth and boundless joy.   1030

—Good fortune in such fine balance
deserves to be treated with respect.

—My lady queen.

CLYTEMNESTRA Step down, Trojan women. Here, take my hand.
Help me put my feet on firm ground.

(*to* ELECTRA)

The temples of the gods have been adorned
with plunder from Troy. As a small but fine reward
for my house, I've chosen living spoils, these women—
petty recompense for a daughter lost.

ELECTRA I, too, am a slave cast out from home   1040
and heritage, consigned to this hovel. So
may I not, Mother, take your royal hand?

CLYTEMNESTRA (*dismounting*)
My slaves are here to spare you work on my account.

ELECTRA Why spare me, held captive far from home?
When I was seized, seized from my home as they were,
I became one of them, fatherless, orphaned.

CLYTEMNESTRA That, I assure you, was your father's doing. He
should not have schemed as he did against his dear ones.
I also say that when a woman forms a wrong opinion,
her tongue turns bitter. In your situation,   1050
one can't fault you. But when the facts are learned,
if you find me worth loathing, then
to hate is right. If not, why do we need to hate?

Tyndareos gave me to your father not
that I should die, nor the children I bore.
But your father, promising my daughter marriage
to Achilles, lured her to Aulis where his ships were
held in irons, and there, racking her on the altar,
he slashed my Iphigenia's white throat.
And if, to avert the city's fall or help   1060
his own family or save other children, he'd killed one
for the sake of many, his act would be excusable.
But as it was, when Helen went mad with lust,

59

Menelaos did nothing to control his faithless wife
and punish her adultery. Then, to counter
such inaction, your father killed my child.
Just for these things—though I was sorely wronged—
I would not have turned savage nor killed my husband.
But then he came home, a raving, god-smitten girl
on his arm, in his bed. Thus did one house   1070
suffer occupation by two brides.

Yes, women can be foolish. I won't deny it.
But granting this, whenever a husband strays
and abandons his marriage bed, the woman wants
to imitate his lead and find her own friend.
Yet censure strikes hard at women, while men,
the true agents of trouble, hear no reproach.
Now, if Menelaos had been swept off in secret,
should I have killed Orestes to save
my sister's husband? And how would your father   1080
have borne his son's death? Should a killer
not be executed? Was I to keep suffering?

I did kill him. Taking the only possible path,
I joined his enemies. Would any of his friends
have aided me in his destruction?
Rebut me, if you must. You are quite free
to tell me that your father died unjustly.

CHORUSLEADER The reasons are just, but *this* justice is ugly.
A woman knows, if she has common sense,
that she defers in all things to her husband.   1090
Else, I cannot count her as a proper wife.

ELECTRA Let me remind you, Mother, that you concluded
your defense with words permitting me frankness.

CLYTEMNESTRA Be frank, child. I won't retract that permission.

ELECTRA But, Mother, will you use what you hear to hurt me?

CLYTEMNESTRA I'll hurt you only with sweet understanding.

ELECTRA Then I have leave to speak. To begin with, Mother,
I wish your understanding were more balanced.
Indeed, the outward beauty you and Helen share
brings well-earned praise, but inside both you sisters are   1100
rotten with lust, unworthy of your brother Castor.
She was ruined by consenting to her own rape,
and you destroyed the best, the finest man in Greece
offering a child's death as your excuse
for killing your husband. But I know you better.

Long before your daughter's sacrifice had been decreed,
but not long after your lord husband sailed for Troy,
you smiled at the mirror teasing your golden hair.
But when a woman whose man is elsewhere struts out
in festive garb, she can be written off as a slut.   1110
A woman should never show the streets her painted face
unless she goes prowling with mischief in mind.
And I know that you alone, of all the Greeks,
tingled with pleasure when the odds favored Troy,
but when Troy's luck turned bad, your eyes gathered clouds,
for you did not desire Agamemnon's safe return.
Yet, you had a fine, fair chance to show restraint.
Your husband was not a man worse than Aigisthos
but a man whom Greece herself chose commander-in-chief.
And when your sister Helen did such fatal harm,   1120
you could have taken on great praise. Vice
gives its lesson as virtue's mirror-image.

But if, as you state, my father killed your daughter,
how have my brother and I done you wrong?
Why, when you'd killed him, were we not deeded
our heritage? Because you used what was not yours
as dowry to pay your bedmate's keep.
Your present husband is not exiled on your son's behalf,
nor has he died for me, though mine is a living
death worse than my killed sister's. And if blood   1130

61

calls for blood in the name of Justice, I will kill you—
I and your son Orestes—to avenge our father.

(stepping back)

If death was just there, here it is also just.
[The man's a fool who, dazzled by her wealth and rank,
marries a worthless schemer. A pauper's bed
that honors chastity is softer than a king's.

CHORUSLEADER Marriage is a woman's gamble. I've seen
the dice fall to bring good luck and bad.]

CLYTEMNESTRA Daughter, by nature you've always loved your father,
and it happens that some children prefer the male parent 1140
while some hold greater fondness for the mother.
I shall excuse you, for I do not find
much reason in my own acts for rejoicing.
Oh how my best intentions went astray when I
drove more passion than I meant against my husband.

ELECTRA Too late to lament. There's no cure now.
My father is dead, dead. Why not call home
the wanderer, your exiled son?

CLYTEMNESTRA I've been afraid to. I look to my good, not his.
They say he's angry at the murder of his father.   1150

ELECTRA Why turn your husband savage against us?

CLYTEMNESTRA It's his way, just as you were born willful.

ELECTRA I'm in pain. But I'll bring my anger to an end.

CLYTEMNESTRA And then he'll no longer be hard on you.

ELECTRA He dreams of greatness while he sprawls in my house.

CLYTEMNESTRA You see? It's you who add new tinder to the quarrel.

ELECTRA I'm *silent,* for I fear him as I do fear him.

CLYTEMNESTRA Stop this talk! Child, why do you want me here?

ELECTRA You heard, I think, that I was brought to bed.
Make the sacrifice for me—I don't know how—   1160
the one required on a child's tenth day.
I'm a new mother with no experience.

CLYTEMNESTRA That's work for the midwife who delivered you.

ELECTRA I delivered myself. I gave birth alone.

CLYTEMNESTRA You live here without friends and neighbors?

ELECTRA A poor working man—no one wants him for a friend.

CLYTEMNESTRA And look at you, unkempt and clad in tatters!
Is this the way you've rested from childbirth?
I'll help. Because the child completes its tenth day,
I'll make the sacrifice. For you, I'll do this favor   1170
before I meet my husband at his own sacrifice
in honor of the Nymphs.

(*to her attendants*)

Stable the horses
and fodder them. And when I have finished
with this little sacrifice, be ready,
for husbands also need their favors.

CLYTEMNESTRA's *attendants exeunt with the horses.*

ELECTRA (*motioning* CLYTEMNESTRA *to precede her into the farmhouse*)

Welcome to my humble house. But take care, please,
not to smudge your finery with clinging soot.
You shall indeed make the sacrifice
as must be done to satisfy the powers of heaven.   1180

63

(*addressing* CLYTEMNESTRA'S *back as she walks to the*
farmhouse)

The basket waits, and the new-whetted knife that killed
the bull. You'll fall beside him when you take your blow.
And you shall be bride again in death's house to him
you lay with while he lived. I will render you this favor,
and you render me just payment for my father.

ELECTRA *follows* CLYTEMNESTRA *into the farmhouse.*

CHORUS (*singing and dancing*)
Exchange for evils! Oh how the winds
of the house turn around. Once my true king
was struck down as he bathed
and massive roof timbers and walls built of marble
all echoed, repeating his deathwails, "You   1190
ingrate! Savage! Woman, why kill me? Dear country—
ten springtimes gone,
at last I've come home."

Just payment reclaims the reckless one
who strayed from her bed not once but again,
when at last he came home
to his city where towers built by giants reach into heaven.
And her hand lifted the weapon, and her hand
chopped the axe down. She killed you, O husband
most grievously wronged   1200
by a faithless wife.
Just like some angry mountain lioness
that leaves her thicket-guarded den, she stalked and struck.

CLYTEMNESTRA (*inside the farmhouse*)
Children! Dear god, I'm your mother! Don't kill me.

CHORUSLEADER (*speaking*) Do you hear—"My god, don't kill me"?

CLYTEMNESTRA NO! NOT ME! NO-O-O-O!

CHORUSLEADER No! Not her! No! Killed by her own children.

CHORUS (*chanting*) God deals just payment as fortune requires.
Savage your death, poor creature, but godless
the death you devised.   1210

CHORUSLEADER (*speaking*)
But they're leaving the house, walking our way,
splashed by their mother's fresh blood.
                                    I want to run
from such unhappy proof of sacrifice.
No family and its many generations
have been more their own victim.

        ELECTRA, ORESTES, *and* PYLADES *enter from the farm-
            house, followed by attendants carrying the bodies of*
                            CLYTEMNESTRA *and* AIGISTHOS.

        The lines from here until CASTOR'S *opening speech are
                                                    chanted.*

ORESTES IO,
Earth and Zeus who sees everything
human, look now on the blood
that defiles me—two bodies   1220
struck to the ground by my hand
as poor reparation
for wrongs I have suffered.

ELECTRA This rush of tears—oh brother, mine the guilt and shame.
On fire, the daughter dared rage at the mother
who gave her birth.

CHORUS Oh fate, your fate, Mother,
when you birthed pain the world
won't forget or forgive and, worse,
were killed by your children's hands.   1230
But, blood for blood, you paid the just price.

65

ORESTES IO,
Apollo, your voice hymned a justice
I could not see clear, but all too clear
the anguish you caused, the bloodhaunted,
homeless future you've doled out.
What nation will have me?
What host, what god-fearing person
will look in the face of a man
who killed his own mother?   1240

ELECTRA And where, oh where shall *I* go? What dancing be mine?
What marriage? What husband will lead me,
a bride, to his bed?

CHORUS Again, again your mind
has changed course with the wind.
For you think now of godly things
ignored when you worked dreadful
deeds on your brother against his will.

ORESTES Did you see how terror made her rip open
her robes exposing her breasts against bloodshed?   1250
How slowly the naked limbs that bore me
sagged to the ground. And I melted away.

CHORUS You walked through anguish, I know,
when you heard the mother who bore you
singing her own dirge.

ORESTES She wailed it, she screamed, she reached up placing
soft begging hands on my cheeks, "My son, my own son!"
and pressed her palms tight on my face
so pity would loosen my grip on the knife.

CHORUS Poor woman. How could you bear   1260
the sight of the mother you murdered
breathing her last breath?

ORESTES I cast my cloak over my eyes.
                                And then I began

the ritual act, loosing
the knife in my mother's neck.

ELECTRA But calling the stroke, my hand on yours, I took
the knife and guided it home. Of most
dreadful suffering, I am the cause.

ORESTES Cover my mother's body with robes,   1270
                              and cleanse her, close
the wounds of sacrifice.
You gave birth to your own death.

ORESTES takes off his cloak and, with ELECTRA'S *help,*
uses it to cover CLYTEMNESTRA'S *body.*

ELECTRA Bear witness for one who is loved and not loved:
we cast the cloak gently around her,
an end of great woe for our house.

As the CHORUS *chants the next lines,* CASTOR *and POLY-*
DEUKES *appear on the roof of the farmhouse.*

CHORUS (*severally*)—But look, up there on the rooftop,
a shimmer of lights.

                   —Who are they,
spirits or gods? No mortal foot walks   1280
the pathway of air.

                   —Why do they show themselves
brightly to human eyes?

CASTOR Agamemnon's son, pay heed. As brothers
to your mother, as twin sons of Zeus, we,
Castor and Polydeukes, claim your attention.
As soon as we had calmed high waves for passing ships,
we came here, for we had perceived
the sacrifice you made—our sister, your mother.
She has her just deserts but by your unjust act.   1290

67

Apollo, Apollo—but he is my lord. I will
keep silence. He is wise forever, though his oracle
spoke brutal words. We are bound to acquiesce.
And you must do now as Fate and Zeus ordain.

First, give Pylades Electra as his bride.
Then, leave Argos. You who killed your mother
may not enter your inheritance, this city.
The terror you called forth, the hounding goddesses of doom,
shall hunt you, driving you here, there, homeless and mad.
But when you stagger into Athens, embrace   1300
the image of Pallas. She shall then lift
her Gorgon shield above your head to keep the spitting
fury of those hideous snakes from touching you.
Nearby you shall find Ares' hill where gods themselves
first cast the votes on a matter of blood when rage
brought Ares' always savage temper to a flash
and he killed the son of the Sea-God for raping
his daughter. Since then, the votes of the court command
utmost respect; its decisions stand firm.
On that spot, pursued, you must be tried for murder,   1310
but votes cast evenly shall save you from being
put to death. Apollo shall take your guilt back on himself
because his oracle foretold your mother's murder.
In the future this shall be law: that the accused
always win acquittal on an even vote.
The baying goddesses shall vanish, thwarted,
when earth beside the hill splits in a holy gape
where men shall afterwards tremble, listening to oracles.
But you must go to live by Arkadia's wild river
near the shrine haunted by Zeus of the Wolves   1320
and there found a city that bears your name.

This is your lot. For Aigisthos, the gods ordain
that citizens shall bury him in native earth.
And your mother shall be honored with a funeral
by Menelaos, now in homeport on return from Troy;
by Helen, too. Leaving her safe retreat, Helen
comes from Egypt. She never went to Troy.

Zeus—yes, Zeus—intending war and slaughtered men
sent only Helen's image to that battleground.
And Pylades—let him receive this maiden-wife   1330
and take her to his home. Let him also lead
your pretended brother-in-law to his city
and there give him wealth beyond his dreams.

As for you, cross the Isthmus and make your way
to Athens' templed hill that gleams with heaven's blessings.
When you have paid as Fate decrees for murder,
heaven shall bless you by releasing you from pain.

The lines from here until ELECTRA *and* PYLADES *exeunt
are chanted.*

ORESTES O sons of Zeus, does heaven grant
        mortal voices the right to address you?

CASTOR You have the right. The blood of sacrifice   1340
       does not defile you.

ELECTRA And I may speak to Tyndareos' sons?

CASTOR You may. I will refer the murder
       back to Apollo.

ORESTES Why, as gods and brothers to her
        who was slain, did you not
        keep Death-Spirits away?

CASTOR Fate and the unwise cry of Apollo
       fulfilled necessity's binding demand.

ELECTRA But when did Apollo—when did his voice   1350
        ever ordain that *I* kill my mother?

CASTOR Deeds in common, destinies in common:
       mother and father,
       one ancestral curse destroyed them both.

ORESTES My sister, whom it took too long to find,
    too soon I am robbed of your love,
    and I shall abandon you, you leave me.

CASTOR A husband is hers, a noble house.
    The girl suffers nothing save leaving
    her country forever.   1360

ELECTRA What greater sorrow than being forced
    to leave behind my native earth?

ORESTES But I, my heritage forever lost,
    must wander till I pay the price
    for a mother's blood.

CASTOR   Take heart. You shall reach
    Athena's city. Exercise patience.

ELECTRA Hold me close, brother, let me hold you.
    Oh how I love you!
    One from the other, both from our home,   1370
    we're torn—cursed by a mother's murder—apart.

ORESTES Hurry, come hold me, though I am dead.
    Shed tears on my body as on my grave.

ELECTRA *and* ORESTES *embrace.*

CASTOR Pain, such pain in your words that even
    gods hear its anguish.
    I and my heavenly kind know
    pity for men who must suffer and die.

ORESTES Never again shall I see you.

ELECTRA Nor I see myself in your eyes.

ORESTES This, the last time I'll talk with you ever.   1380

70

ELECTRA O my homeland, goodbye.
         Goodbye to you, women of home.

ORESTES Most loyal of sisters, do you leave now?

ELECTRA I leave with tears blurring all that I see.

ORESTES Pylades, go. I wish you all joy
         in Electra your bride.

                        ELECTRA *and* PYLADES *exeunt.*

CASTOR (*speaking*)
        Marriage awaits them. But you, run! The hounds
        snap fierce at your heels. Turn toward Athens.
        I hear them pelting hard on you, I see
        black flesh and snake-hands coiling   1390
        round a fruit of agonizing pain.

                        ORESTES, *panicked, exits.*

        Ships are breaking in high seas off Sicily.
        Our immediate presence is required. But first,
        let me tell you we speed through wide air
        not to rescue those whom murder pollutes
        but those who hold precious in life all things
        godly and just. Such are the people
        we save when we hear of their peril.
        Let none of you, then, commit an injustice
        or go aboard ship with perjured men.   1400
        As a god, I give warning to you who must die.

                    CASTOR *and* POLYDEUKES *exeunt.*

CHORUS I wish you joy. To spend life's fleeting days
        mid joy that never meets an evil hour
        is to be blessed beyond compare.

                        The CHORUS *exits slowly.*

A NOTE ON STAGING

The scene shows a farmhouse, with perhaps a statue of Apollo in front of it and an altar. It is a poor, isolated farm in the uplands. No clear stage directions are given for the many places of offstage action mentioned in the text, which include:

the Farmer's fields
a spring
Orestes' country of exile (= Pylades' homeland)
Agamemnon's tomb
the city of Argos
the Old Man's encampment
fields where Aigisthos sacrifices to the Nymphs
a barn in which Clytemnestra's horses are stabled
Athens

Let the Farmer's fields lie in the one direction, stage left. Then the spring will lie in the other direction (stage right); and so, further on, will Aigisthos' fields, Agamemnon's tomb, and the great town of Mycenae on the Argive plain (which Euripides rather casually identifies with the modern town of Argos). Orestes and the Old Man enter from the same direction as the tomb, which lies well outside the town. Orestes will depart for Athens in the opposite direction from which he came.

NOTES ON THE TEXT

1–54 *Age-old valley . . . he's the fool* The prologue begins with well-known material: Agamemnon's victory at Troy, his murder by Clytemnestra his wife and her lover Aigisthos, the latter's illegitimate rule, the sending away of the child Orestes (here smuggled out by an old retainer) to Strophios, king of Phokis. The new, surprising additions concern Electra. In this version she is "married" to the Farmer, but their marriage has not been consummated. This makes Electra a dangerous, liminal figure, between virgin and wife.

9–10 *he was killed . . . Aigisthos* Reports differ on how this was done, and by whom. In Homer, Agamemnon is trapped and killed by Aigisthos, with Clytemnestra's help; in Aeschylus, by Clytemnestra, backed by Aigisthos; in Euripides, by Aigisthos, driven by Clytemnestra (though at ll. 1198–99 [Greek text 1159–60] the chorus has her kill Agamemnon herself, with an axe, not the usual sword). By their suggestive word order lines 9–10 make it clear that Clytemnestra's cunning (*dolōi*) is the active force behind the murder, Aigisthos' hand her instrument. Here, as elsewhere, Aigisthos is referred to as "Thyestes' son" in the Greek, recalling family guilt and revenge (see the introduction).

15–18 *the baby Orestes . . . protection* A mere babe when Agamemnon left for Troy, Orestes is now a strapping youth of eighteen or nineteen. Electra is somewhat older. In Sophocles' version, she had mothered the child Orestes and had herself arranged to have him sent away from Argos. Who, to Euripides' mind, would have taken that initiative? Agamemnon's old retainer? Or, just possibly, Clytemnestra?

25–28 *Yet, when he planned . . . Aigisthos' hand* The innovation is significant. Clytemnestra, though raw-minded, yet prevents Aigisthos from killing her daughter. She is capable of pity, and of remorse.

29 *Clytemnestra had excuses*   These were: first, Agamemnon's sacrifice of their daughter Iphigenia, so the ships could sail from Aulis to Troy; second, and less cogent, his bringing home the Trojan prophetess Cassandra as his mistress.

43 *Aigisthos would have paid the penalty*   The word *dikē* is central. We translate it variously by vengeance, justice, a just price, judgment, and just payment.

61 *Tyndareos' daughter*   This refers to Clytemnestra, daughter of Leda and Tyndareos, but it could equally refer to her half-sister Helen, Zeus' daughter in fact, Tyndareos' daughter by courtesy. Euripides often connects the sisters as bearers of ruin.

63 *home and heritage*   We use this phrase to translate *oikos* (house, home, family), as here, and *domos patrōios* (ancestral house) elsewhere.

91 *He ordered me home*   This is implied in the Greek but not precisely stated. In Aeschylus, Orestes says more about Apollo's bidding and the dire threats accompanying it should Orestes fail to avenge his father. In Sophocles the oracle's advice is ambiguous and perhaps deceptive.

110–12 *Look, here comes . . . somebody's slave*   These lines supply retroactive stage directions. Electra's cropped hair, her ragged clothes, and the water-jar she carries mark her clearly (and misleadingly) as a slave.

115–71 *Speed your step . . . lie in her bed*   Electra's sung lament will stir the audience's sympathy and will make a strong impression on the listening Orestes. She *has* suffered, she *has* many reasons for her continued mourning, and any hints that her grief is excessive, or that she is alienated from society, are subtle as yet.

142–43 ELECTRA *takes the water-jar*   She might have called an attendant to take it. More likely, she self-consciously directs her own actions.

171–72 *The* CHORUS *enters*   These are young, unmarried women who live in the uplands, remote from town, eager for gossip and for special occasions like Hera's festival. Their bright clothing, cheerfulness, and sociability make a powerful contrast with Electra's appearance, mourning, and isolation.

179 *at Hera's temple*   Hera was goddess of marriage as well as patron of Argos. The Heraia festival, celebrated at her temple between Argos and Mycenae, included athletic contests and military displays; its high point was probably a representation of the sacred marriage of Hera and Zeus.

229–30 ORESTES, PYLADES A scene of only partial recognition. Electra, afraid at first of bandits, is delighted to find that the "stranger" brings word from Orestes; but the "stranger," apart from revealing that Orestes lives, evades Electra's direct questions and redirects her thoughts to her own situation of pain, grief, and indignity, which she exaggerates for the benefit of the "absent" Orestes. The latter tries rather lamely to conceal his strong emotion—and strong self-concern.

231 *Apollo* Electra may turn to an actual statue of Apollo before her cottage. If such exists, it will remind us of Apollo's presence behind the scenes, sanctioning (rightly or wrongly) the forthcoming murders.

270 *Only Orestes has that right* If a woman's father was dead or missing, she would normally be given in marriage by her new *kyrios* (legal guardian), the nearest male relative.

283 *Are they your friends* As often happens in Euripides' plays, the chorus will keep silence in order to help the main character(s). In so doing, they will become accomplices of the revenge.

292 *from my mother's throat* Forms of the verb *sphattō* (to cut the throat) are ordinarily used of animal sacrifice. In *Electra* they are applied often, and significantly, to the killing of human victims.

324–25 *and stand ashamed before Castor . . . my own kind* Castor and Polydeukes, the Dioskouroi, were sons of Zeus and Leda, brothers of Helen, half-brothers of Clytemnestra, uncles of Electra and Orestes. Together with a few other privileged demigods, including Heracles and Dionysos, they were admitted to Olympos. A probably later variant makes Castor mortal and Polydeukes immortal; the twins share their fate, spending six months in Hades, six on Olympos. It seems that, in the old days, Electra was courted by Castor and might have expected to marry him.

373 [*Take in their gear.*] The line [Greek text 360] has been thought spurious, but needlessly: the Farmer is not dirt poor, and he would naturally have slaves. With self-mocking humor he refers to his "attendants," and to the "gates" of his domain. (We take *tōnde* to refer to Orestes and Pylades (these people's baggage); it is possible, however, that the Farmer addresses *their* attendants, including a servant who will reappear as messenger, line 787.)

381–404 *There's no precise mark . . . courage* Orestes' rather lengthy remarks on nobility reflect contemporary discussions at Athens: Is nobility (*eugeneia*) inherited or learned? How best can it be fostered? And (Orestes' main concern) how can inner nobility be discerned as against mere outward semblances? Compare the interest of Boccaccio and Chaucer in discussions of what constitutes true *gentilezza* or *gentilesse*.

387–93 *How does one find . . . speculation* These seven lines [Greek text 373–79] are bracketed by Diggle as possible interpolations. We argue that the truisms (1) are in character for Orestes, (2) cover his hesitation, and (3) challenge the audience to form its own judgment—about the "noble" Orestes, among others.

400–404 [*Such people bring credit . . . courage*] These lines [Greek text 386–90], also bracketed by Diggle, seem less relevant, and more farfetched, than lines 387–93 [Greek text 373–79] but they bear ironically on the evaluation of Orestes, who is characterized at least metaphorically as a successful athlete.

448–502 CHORUS While time, by the usual convention, goes forward in the outer world during the singing and dancing of this choral ode, the chorus moves backward, singing (1) how Achilles came to Troy, (2) how (before that) he received his divinely made arms, and (3) how (before that) he was brought up by the good centaur Chiron.

468–95 *And I heard . . . black dust* The audience will recall Homer's description in *Iliad* 18 of the great shield made for Achilles by Hephaistos, with its typical, contrasting scenes of war and peace. The figures on Euripides' armor are fearful and portentous, intended to dazzle the eyes of the Trojans and especially those of Hector, the Trojan champion (who would be killed by Achilles). They include: (1) Perseus slaying the Gorgon, with Hermes' help; (2) the murderous Sphinx, here not overcome, and (3) Bellerophon riding the winged horse Pegasos, to attack the monstrous Chimaera. The first group foreshadows, and is foil to, Orestes' killing of Clytemnestra. Compare Aeschylus' *Libation Bearers* (ll. 832–37), where the chorus urges Orestes (who is inside) to "take up the heart of Perseus" in his breast and to "kill the evil Gorgon by spreading a cloak" before his eyes so he won't be turned to stone. It is all right to look as he kills Aigisthos. Euripides will develop this comparison, with bitter irony.

503 OLD MAN He had been Agamemnon's *tropheus* (ll. 17, 425) [Greek text 16, 409] and *paidagōgos*, not just a tutor in the modern sense, but a male nursemaid, companion, and guide.

529–31 *And there on the altar . . . someone's head* The recognition-signs here rejected by Electra are taken from Aeschylus' *Libation Bearers* (ll. 164–234), where Electra discovers (1) a lock of hair at the tomb, like hers, that Orestes might have laid there—or sent; (2) footprints matching hers—as she demonstrates by experiment. When Orestes reveals himself, after that, he adds (3) a piece of Electra's weaving that he had kept with him all those years. Full recognition quickly ensues.

570–71 *To which of your friends . . . belong* Orestes assumes, with typical snobbery, that the Old Man is a slave. Compare his quick assumption earlier that Electra must be married to some low ditchdigger or cowherd.

591 *The scar over his eyebrow* This is evidently Euripides' invention. It is played off against the scar of Odysseus that Eurykleia, the old nurse, recognizes when she is bathing "the stranger" in *Odyssey* 19—but Odysseus forces her to keep silence, and Athena diverts Penelope's mind and vision elsewhere so that she fails, at least consciously, to perceive her husband's presence, and the expected recognition is delayed. The Homeric scar, inflicted by a wild boar, was emblematic of Odysseus' initiation into heroic manhood. In Euripides' play, Orestes' scar (Why didn't Electra notice it earlier?) belongs to a less heroic world. (In Sophocles' *Electra*, Orestes more appropriately displays their father's signet ring.)

638 *I've come for just this crown* This is one of many allusions to the great Games of Hellas, where victors were crowned with wreaths. In a happier world Orestes would have been a star athlete, not a matricide. Killing is played off against sport. Later on, Aigisthos will be fooled by Orestes' pretense of being a Thessalian gentleman en route to Olympia. In Sophocles' *Electra*, Aigisthos and Clytemnestra are fooled by the story that Orestes was accidentally killed in a chariot race at Delphi.

649 *Preparing a feast* The Nymphs were protectors of family life. One might make sacrifices to them in gratitude for existing children or in the hope of children yet to come.

671 *I myself will arrange* Or, reading *exaitēsomai*, "I will ask the privilege of my mother's murder" (Denniston). A quick, confident, cold-blooded assertion—either way.

674 *As you wish* If the Old Man spoke this line, as seems probable, then line 675 [Greek text 651] ("Go to Clytemnestra") becomes unnecessary. If Orestes spoke it, then Electra's turning to the Old Man, giving blunt directions and ignoring Orestes until line 692 [Greek text 668] is all the more striking.

678 *postpartum rites* This refers to the purification ceremony by which the mother was reintegrated into normal society after childbirth. The naming of the child took place on the same tenth day.

682 *She'll come* Electra's tone is cold, sarcastic. She believes that Clytemnestra, once having heard of the newborn child, will come out of curiosity and concern, perhaps wanting to ascertain that it is truly lowborn.

694–95 ORESTES, ELECTRA, *and the* OLD MAN *pray* The order of speakers is uncertain. Following Denniston's lead, we give line 698 [Greek text 674] to Electra, who would appropriately invoke the goddess Hera; but we also give her line 704 [Greek text 680], for dramatic symmetry.

702 *(kneeling and beating on the ground)* The stage directions are inferred from the text, not supplied by it. For a Greek audience, they would help recall the great invocation scene in Aeschylus' *Libation Bearers*.

707–20 *You, forever wronged . . . waiting* Our arrangement of lines 707–20, following Diggle, leaves many problems inadequately solved. It may be preferable, as David Kovacs suggests, (1) to restore line 708 [Greek text 684] to Electra, who cuts ceremony short with her usual abruptness; (2) to bracket lines 714–18 [Greek text 688–92], not 711–15 [Greek text 685–89], as an otiose attempt to explain and expand upon 712–13 [Greek text 686–87], and (3) to restore line 709 [Greek text 693] to its place after 718 [Greek text 692] but divide it between Orestes ("I get it") and Electra, who speaks first to Orestes ("Be the man . . .") and then to the chorus.

724–71 *How tender . . . murdered your husband* Once again the choral ode covers the passing of time while the murder of Aigisthos is being carried out. It refers, somewhat one-sidedly, to Thyestes' adultery with Aerope, wife of his brother Atreus, and her conveying to him the Golden Lamb, emblem of divinely ordained kingship; there is no mention of Atreus' horrible vengeance ("Thyestes' Feast"), an even more likely cause of the heavenly portents.

752–61 *Then thunder boomed . . . lifeless desert* In other versions, the sun reversed his course only temporarily, whether from horror or to confirm Atreus' rightful kingship. The present, apparently unique version makes him change his course to drive westward, as he has done *ever since*. Oddly enough, this change is accompanied by another reversal, of north (to be wet) and south (dry).

768–69 *And stories that strike fear . . . the gods* The young women of the chorus, who have grown somewhat sophisticated since the last choral ode, hint at an "opiate of the people" theory that was held by, among others, the oligarch Kritias (ca. 460–403 B.C.) In this view, religion was invented by a few clever people to enforce a general fear of unseen transgressions.

772 *EA! EA!* These inarticulate cries are transliterated from the Greek.

787 *Now let winning* The messenger proclaims victory, as in battle or an athletic contest, for the "maidens of Mycenae" through their champion Orestes (*kallinikoi* 787 [Greek text 761], picked up at 894 [865], 911 [880]). Other athletic comparisons are given at 852–53 [824–25], 901–3 [862–65], 912–21 [880–85], and 987–90 [954–56].

799 *How did Aigisthos die?* In Greek he is "Thyestes' son," recalling the ancient feud. There is also a play on *Thyestes* and *thyein* (to sacrifice).

820–21 *But Orestes tells him . . . for the gods* To avoid possible contamination of the sacrifice, the stranger is invited to wash his hands; but Orestes refuses, "presumably because that would make him a full participant in the religious ceremony and involve him in sacrilege" (Denniston). His subsequent behavior shows fewer scruples.

827–72 *Some carried bowls . . . died hard* Euripides describes ritual sacrifice both as it should be and as, in this instance, it is perverted into murder.

855 *took the innards* Aigisthos practices haruspicy (the inspection of an animal's entrails for good or bad signs), and he discovers warning of a truly approaching danger. Orestes reassures him, with splendid irony.

885 *they put a crown* This is the victory garland (*stephanos*) for the head of a military or athletic victor. Electra will shortly crown the heads of Orestes and Pylades (ll.901–3, 912–21 [Greek text 870–72, 880–89])—and insult the head of the dead Aigisthos.

928 *I give you his head* Or, literally, "I bring you the dead man himself." Euripides gives hints, perhaps (especially at ll. 885–87 [Greek text 855–57]), but no clear stage directions here; we take full responsibility for separating Aigisthos' head from the rest of his body, despite the strong arguments of David Kovacs (*Classical Philology* 82 [1987], 139–41).

935 *Except censure* Speaking ill of the dead ran contrary to strongly held Greek custom. Electra's insults to Aigisthos' corpse are represented as *hybris*, on a par with Aigisthos' insults, reported earlier by Electra, to Agamemnon's corpse and tomb.

941–90 *Where to begin . . . life's last lap* Electra's insults tumble out without plan or structure, conveying the vehemence of her loathing for the dead Aigisthos.

966–69 *Sheer disgrace . . . the mother's* Although Greek households were male-centered, a wife's high birth and rich dowry could give her more than usual authority. Electra's antifeminist comments are especially inappropriate in the mouth of this domineering daughter of a domineering mother.

996–1022 *Stop! Enough! . . . not sweet* The tension of the following scene, in which Electra pushes Orestes to be bloody, bold, and resolute, is enhanced by the already visible and audible approach of Clytemnestra with her entourage. Notice the great emphasis, by turn, on the words "mother" and "father."

1019 *with Aigisthos' help* We read *Aigisthou meta* (with Aigisthos: Wilamowitz) or, still better, *Aigisthou cheri* (by Aigisthos' hand: Parmentier; and compare ll. 10, 16 [17]). Orestes should kill Clytemnestra by a trick, as she killed Agamemnon, using Aigisthos as a helper or instrument—which is, ironically, how Electra is using Orestes now.

1029–32 *You merit reverence . . . respect* The chorus praises Clytemnestra in exaggerated terms that should elicit the gods' resentment (*phthonos*). This closely recalls the scene in Aeschylus' *Agamemnon* where Clytemnestra pressed Agamemnon to tread on the red carpet of precious cloths.

1047–87 *That, I assure you* Clytemnestra's remarks open what becomes virtually a defendant's plea in a court trial; we know that she has already been condemned without a hearing and that the executioner is waiting within. Trial scenes of this kind (*agōnes*) were common in Euripides' plays, exciting for the audience and a means of exploring, though not solving, complex issues of moral choice and responsibility. Generally, as here, the second speaker successfully refutes the first.

1050 *In your situation* Other readings and interpretations of this line [Greek text 1015] are possible: (1) In our situation, this is understandable (reading, *hēmin, ou kakōs*); (2) In my view, this is not well done (*hēmin, ou kalōs*). In either case, Clytemnestra argues that, once the facts are known, the prejudice against her must disappear.

1069 *a raving god-smitten girl*   This is Cassandra, Apollo's prophetess, who foretold Troy's fall but never was believed. Agamemnon brought her back to Argos as his mistress.

1121–22 *vice gives its lesson* . . . *mirror-image*   Electra means that, for good people, the wicked behavior of others gives negative examples of what they should avoid. There is also a typically Euripidean suggestion that the example of vice is infectious, a powerful miseducation.

1134–38 *The man's a fool* . . . *good luck and bad*   These lines [Greek text 1097–1101] have been deleted by some editors as anticlimactic and even silly, but they serve an important dramatic purpose. Electra has come very near the brink of telling the truth, frightening her mother away. Now she steps back, into commonplaces (angry speeches frequently end with such generalizations), and the chorus quickly seconds her move.

1145 *against my husband*   Or, alternatively, "drove my husband [= Aigisthos] to anger," a reflection that Electra may pick up sarcastically at line 1151 [Greek text 1116].

1157 *I do fear him*   The irony is strong, and Electra again runs the risk of frightening her mother away.

1167–68 *And look at you* . . . *childbirth*   With Diggle, we accept Weil's transposition of these lines [Greek text 1107–08] to this place. Clytemnestra seems to see her daughter for the first time: a typical occurrence in this play of moral blindness.

1197 *towers built by giants*   The great Mycenaean walls, of Cyclopean masonry, were supposedly built by the Kyklopes, huge one-eyed giants.

1217 *IO*   Another direct transliteration, pronounced "EE-OH."

1256–58 *she reached up* . . . *on my face*   This is the gesture not only of a mother but also a suppliant, regularly honored by the gods.

1276 *an end of great woe*   The Greek text of this line [1232: following Diggle, we give this to Orestes] is equally ambiguous: woe "has ended" or "has come into its fullness" with Clytemnestra's death.

1276–77 CASTOR *and* POLYDEUKES *appear*   In addition to their family connection (see note on ll. 324–25), the Dioskouroi sometimes appear as bright stars or flames on ships' rigging, a sign of hope and salvation.

1298–1321 *The terror you called forth . . . bears your name* The Furies will pursue Orestes to Athens, where he will be tried before the divinely established court of the Areopagos and acquitted. So much is reassuringly Aeschylean. But notice that (1) the court is not established for Orestes' sake—or the rule that "equal votes spell acquittal"; (2) the Furies will not be reconciled, this time, by Athena's gentle persuasion (in Euripides' *Iphigenia in Tauris* [ll. 968–82], only half the Furies are reconciled, and half continue to pursue Orestes); and (3) Orestes will not reenter his city as its rightful heir and ruler but will found Orestheion, a savage, remote village in Arkadia.

1304 *Ares' hill* Halirrhothios, the son of Poseidon, raped Ares' daughter Alkippe; Ares killed him in anger, was tried for murder by a divinely instituted court, and was acquitted. Thus the Areopagos (Ares' hill) lends its name to the ancient and once-powerful Athenian court that, in Euripides' time, still tried homicide cases.

1327 *She never went to Troy* In the lovely, unorthodox version told by the sixth-century lyric poet Stesichoros and used by Euripides himself in his *Helen* of 412 B.C., Helen was innocent; she remained in, or was sent to, Egypt; and the Trojan war was fought for her image. On the one hand, this means forgiveness for Helen and perhaps, by implication, for all of us. On the other hand, the mystery of evil, of suffering, is referred back to Zeus.

1338–54 *O sons of Zeus . . . destroyed them both* For the choice and order of speakers here (Orestes and Electra, not the chorus, speaking with the Dioskouroi), we follow the manuscript readings [for Greek text 1292–1307], defended by David Kovacs (*Classical Quarterly* 35 [1985], 310–14). If Kovacs's reading of lines 1340–41 [Greek text 1294] is correct, the Dioskouroi are behaving like very liberal justices, indeed, for Castor asserts that Orestes and Electra are not polluted.

1392–93 *Ships are breaking . . . required* Castor's mention of their hurrying to the Sicilian Sea [Greek text 1347–48] has often been taken as an allusion to the Sicilian Expedition of 415–413 B.C., and specifically to Demosthenes' relief expedition in the spring of 413. But this seems overprecise. It is enough that Euripides alludes to perils of nature and history to which cities, not just individuals, must be exposed.

GLOSSARY

ACHILLES: the greatest Greek warrior at Troy; he killed Hector and was killed eventually by Paris.

AIGISTHOS: vengeful son of Thyestes and lover of Clytemnestra, with whom he conspired to kill Agamemnon.

AGAMEMNON: king of Mycenae, leader of the expedition against Troy. He was the husband of Clytemnestra and the father of Iphigenia, Electra, and Orestes.

APHRODITE: goddess of love. She supported Paris and the Trojans.

APOLLO: god of healing, music, and prophecy. His most famous oracle was at Delphi.

ARES: god of war. His hill at Athens, the Areopagos, gave its name to an ancient, revered law court.

ARGIVE: a citizen of Argos.

ARGOS: a city (and also a district) in southern Greece. Euripides uses it interchangeably with Mycenae, capital of Agamemnon.

ARKADIA: a mountainous region in southern Greece.

ATREUS: king of Mycenae, father of Agamemnon and Menelaos, brother of Thyestes and uncle of Aigisthos.

AULIS: ancient port from which the Greek ships sailed to Troy after the sacrifice of Iphigenia.

CASTOR: twin brother of Polydeukes. The two Dioskouroi, sons of Leda and Zeus or Tyndareos, were deified; they often saved sailors from shipwreck.

CLYTEMNESTRA: queen of Mycenae, wife and murderess of Agamemnon.

DELPHI: a holy site in central Greece, home of the oracle of Apollo and the Pythian games.

DIONYSOS: god of wine, madness, and theatrical transformations.

ELECTRA: daughter of Agamemnon and Clytemnestra.

GORGON: one of three sisters, killed by Perseus. Her name was Medusa, and her snake-haired head, even after death, turned beholders to stone.

HECTOR: champion of Troy, killed by Achilles.

HELEN: daughter of Zeus and Leda, half-sister of Clytemnestra, and wife of Menelaos. Her elopement with Paris started the Trojan war.

HEPHAISTOS: god of the forge, patron of early technology. He made divine armor for Achilles at Thetis' request.

HERA: queen of the gods, patroness of Argos.

HERMES: the messenger god, helper of heroes and tricksters.

HYADES: "the rainy ones," five stars in Taurus.

IPHIGENIA: daughter of Agamemnon and Clytemnestra. Her father sacrificed her at Aulis to Artemis so that the Greek ships might sail to Troy. In some versions of the tale, a hind was substituted for her at the last moment.

MENELAOS: king of Sparta, brother of Agamemnon.

MYCENAE: ancient capital of Agamemnon, in the vicinity of Argos.

NAUPLIA: a town in Argos.

ORESTES: son of Clytemnestra and the murdered Agamemnon. As a young boy he was smuggled away to Phokis, the kingdom of his relative Strophios.

OSSA: a mountain in Thessaly.

PAN: a god of flocks and wild places.

PEGASOS: a winged horse, sprung from the Gorgon's blood.

PELION: another mountain in Thessaly.

PERSEUS: son of Zeus and Danae, and one of the most successful of heroes. Among other feats, he killed the Gorgon Medusa.

PHOIBOS: "the bright one," an epithet of Apollo.

PLEIADES: a constellation of seven stars, sometimes pictured as doves.

POLYDEUKES: twin brother of Castor; perhaps better known by his Roman name of Pollux.

PRIAM: king of Troy.

PYLADES: son of Strophios, bosom-friend of Orestes, and eventual husband of Electra.

SPARTA: kingdom of Tyndareos and Menelaos in southern Greece.

SPHINX: a dangerous monster with a human, usually female, head and the body of a lion.

STROPHIOS: ruler of Phokis, brother-in-law of Agamemnon and father of Pylades.

TANTALOS: father of Pelops, founder of the unhappy House of Atreus.

THESSALY: a broad horse-breeding region in northern Greece.

THETIS: a Nereid or sea-nymph, sometime wife of the mortal Peleus and mother of Achilles.

THYESTES: brother and rival of Atreus and father of Aigisthos.

TROY: a city in northwestern Asia Minor.

TYNDAREOS: king of Sparta, father of Helen and Clytemnestra (each of whom may be called Tyndaris).

ZEUS: king of the gods, final arbiter in human affairs.